A Camera in a Room

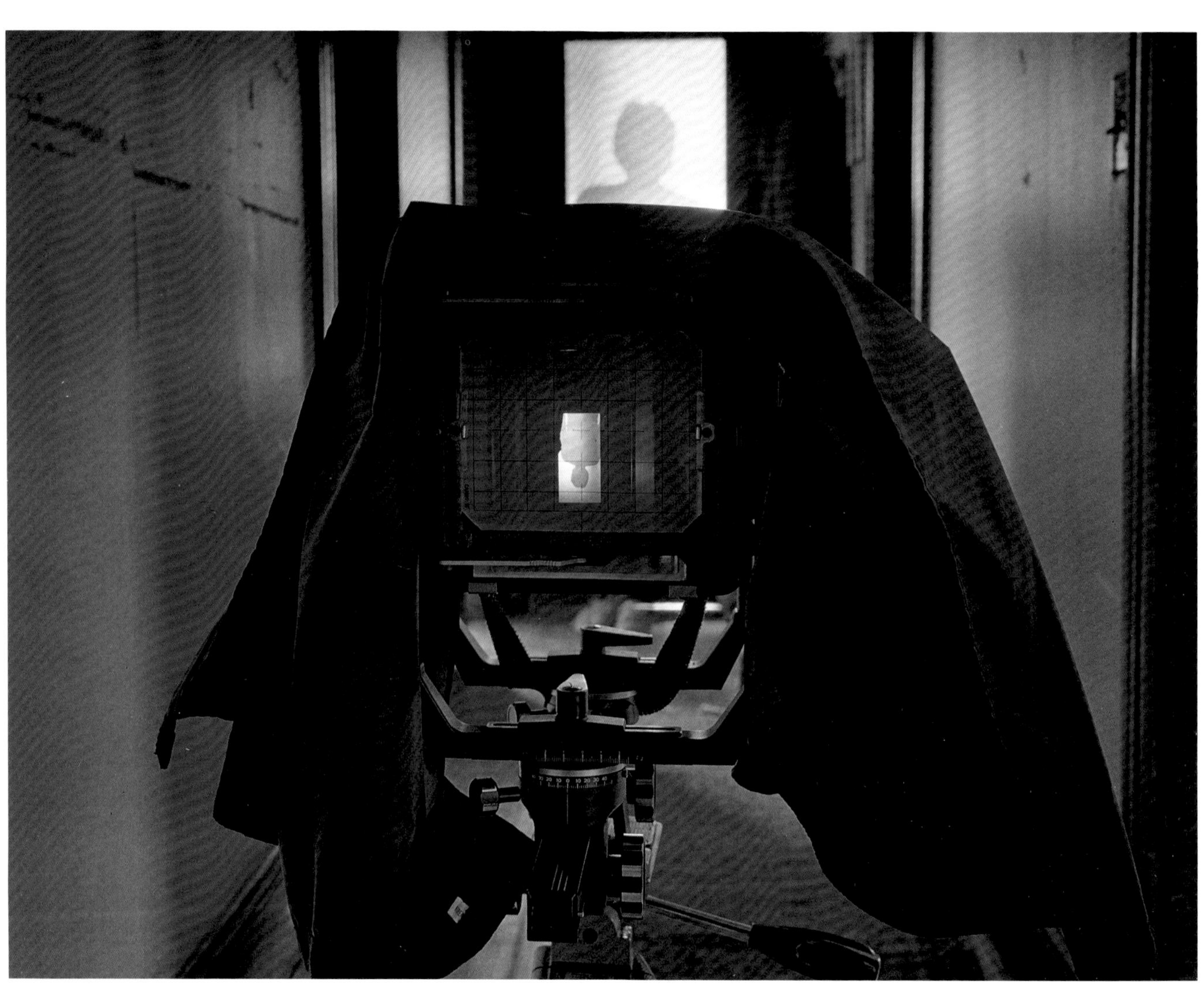

A Camera in a Room

Photographs by Abelardo Morell

Smithsonian Institution Press, Washington and London
Published in association with Constance Sullivan Editions

This series was developed and produced for the Smithsonian Institution Press
by Constance Sullivan Editions

Series editor:
Constance Sullivan

Smithsonian editor:
Amy Pastan

Designed by Katy Homans

Library of Congress Cataloging-in-Publication Data

Morell, Abelardo.
A Camera in a room: photographs / by Abelardo Morell: [edited by Constance Sullivan].
p. cm. —(Photographers at work)
"Published in association with Constance Sullivan Editions."
ISBN 1-56098-548-8 (paper)
1. Photography, Artistic. 2. Morell, Abelardo. I. Sullivan, Constance.
II. Title. III. Series.
TR654.M6383 1995
779'.092—dc20 95-34807
CIP

The paper used in this publication meets the minimum requirements of the
American National Standard for Permanence of Paper for Printed Library Materials
Z39.48–1984.

First edition

Printed by Meridian Printing, East Greenwich, RI, USA

Frontispiece: My Camera and Me, 1991
Cover: Camera Obscura Image of the Empire State Building in Bedroom, 1994

Photographs courtesy of the photographer and Bonni Benrubi Gallery, New York City.

Where did you grow up and how did you get started in photography?

I was born in Cuba and came to the United States with my parents and sister as refugees in 1962, when I was fourteen. We moved to New York and after graduating from high school I got a scholarship to go to Bowdoin College in Maine. Being a Cuban in Maine at that time seemed pretty strange, and although I wanted to fit in it wasn't easy because I felt isolated and scared. I was planning to be an engineer until I flunked freshman physics. That's when I took a photography course, and the first roll of pictures I developed amazed me. For the first time I could express some of the alienation I was feeling.

What were you taking pictures of?

Crazy stuff, like nuns against motorcycles and flying cats, which I printed super contrasty and then would often solarize or step on the print. I didn't know what surrealism was at that time, but my pictures were probably about things not making sense. Photography gave me a personal voice for the first time.

My parents never talked about how unreal it was coming to this country. As difficult as it was, the idea was to survive. Around that time I discovered Robert Frank's book, *The Americans*, and started looking at the work of Diane Arbus and Cartier-Bresson. Their pictures had a poetry of the individual looking at the world and that struck a chord in me. I learned from them that straight photography could pack more surrealism into a picture than I could paste onto one.

Was there one picture you took that indicated what could be done with this medium?

There was a picture of a little girl in a bike shop with a calendar in the background. She had this possessed look in her eyes and the light falling on her was great. I felt, "Oh my God, I've never seen anything like this." And the fact that I had a camera and could name the moment gave me such a sense of power. Maybe it's not such a good picture, but it led me to experience something that I couldn't have experienced without the camera. One of the most interesting things about photography is that it lets you say "I'm aware of this." And you can act on it on the spot.

Did you decide to become a photographer at Bowdoin?

I took a course there with a photographer who was a fantastic teacher. His name is John McKee. He encouraged me and became like a father to me. He was the first to recognize that I had some kind of ambition and talent. Without McKee, I don't think I would have pursued being an artist. After college, I kept photographing with a 35mm camera in the street, mostly in New York but also in Miami, where I went to explore the "Cuban me." In 1979, I went to Yale for my M.F.A. and continued to do a lot—maybe too much—street work.

When did you break from that style?

When my first child, Brady, was born, in 1986, my whole life changed. I remember feeling really depressed that I had to stay home a lot and I literally couldn't go and photograph on the street. One day, as I was leaving home, I saw my wife and son against the glass of a door. It was a pretty sentimental picture, but I made it anyway. I thought, 'People in New York or at Yale will hate it,' but it was my house and I was a father so I gave myself permission to work in this new territory. That led to a whole series of pictures at home, seeing the world through my son's eyes. I had a new landscape to play in. I felt like a kid again, crawling around on the floor. The work I've done ever since has come out of the same sense of curiosity, seeing a book as though it were a mountain. I owe my son a lot for that. He doesn't know it but I do. I also owe my wife for her support, especially when things weren't working out, and she knows it.

What led to the camera obscura pictures?

I teach photography at the Massachusetts College of Art and every year I show beginning students something of the early principles of optics by turning a classroom into a camera obscura. Camera obscuras have been used since before the Renaissance to bring images from the outside into darkened rooms. When my students see projections of people on Huntington Avenue walking upside down on the classroom walls, their reaction is always total amazement that something this low tech could be so magical. Anyway, in 1991, I had a sabbatical from teaching and somehow I got the idea to make photographs of the phenomenon I'd been showing in class.

How do you go about making the pictures?

Basically, I cover all the windows in a room with black plastic so that the room is totally dark. Then I make a hole about 3/8" looking out on some interesting view. What happens is that through this small opening a fairly sharp, upside-down image of the outdoors appears on the wall opposite the hole. It helps if the wall is a light color. After a few minutes in the dark, I'm able to see pretty clearly stuff happening outside now blending with the room. Then, I get my view camera and focus on the projection on the wall. It has to be sunny when I make these pictures and even then the exposures need to be eight hours long. When I first started, it took me half a summer to figure out exposure time and what the best hole size should be.

And every time I got a room ready for a camera obscura picture, my wife and son would witness it. I remember lying in bed with them watching neighbors going to work and squirrels walking on telephone poles. That summer I felt that I had touched on something very important: that the very basics of photography could be potent and strange. So why not make pictures about the medium itself and see where they would take me?

What's the failure rate?

I've made about a dozen camera obscura pictures in all, five of which I like a lot. Some of them were technical failures. On a couple of attempts, the filters on the windows of some New York office buildings reduced the exposure by about a stop and a half. Other images were just not surprising. They looked like cheap surrealism.

How about the light bulb picture?

That actually preceded the camera obscura work. I wanted to make a picture about the way a camera sees to show at school. When I finally got a print I liked I said, "Wow! This is perfect!" It's what photography is all about. This picture gave me the feeling that photography in many ways is still raw and unexplored. Making this picture was for me a way to rediscover the mystery of the medium and maybe to share it with others.

You work on several bodies of pictures at the same time: the pictures of your son and childhood, of the camera obscura, of water and other domestic objects, and of books.

Since I've had kids I find I like being around the house and its interesting to me to try to make photographs of the most ordinary things that I live with. For me, that's the challenge right now. And sometimes one kind of picture leads to another—water suggests optics and optics suggests reflections off the page of a book.

What I love about the book pictures is that you have shown me for the first time, what an artificial, odd construction an illustration in a book really is. You've shown that in many respects: What happens to pictures because of the bending of the pages, the gutters and the leaves, and how the ink of reproductions can give a glossy, mirror-like quality to an image. Of course, at some level, everyone who reads knows this. But I think you were the first to really notice this in a photograph.

I think we know it as children. When you're a child, everything is open for investigation. If you care about something and you look at it, it's bound to change. When I go to libraries now I look at books as physical objects. I turn them around, check out the binding. One of the nice things about books is that they're private. You take a book home and you're free to experience it any way you want. You go to a museum and the pictures are usually structured so there's really only one view of them.

Your pictures of the Caravaggio and the El Greco look solarized but they're not, just as your camera obscura pictures look like sandwich-negatives but they're not: straight photography that looks manipulated.

Right. That gives me a certain amount of pleasure. The postmodern disdain for straight photography always bothered me. Also, what I like about the El Greco *Pietà* is that there's a succession of events implicit in the picture. Whether you are a believer or not, it seems that someone important died in Christianity; then later, El Greco, with that feeling, made a painting of it; then a photographer took a picture of that painting and later someone made a book and decided to reproduce it across two pages of that book; and still later, I look at it and, I hope, retain in my photograph of it, the original spirit that started this chain of events. I don't want to give the photograph a heavy religious connotation, but when Christ turns negative there is a certain transformation having to do with light. I didn't know that at the time but when I see the photograph now I think, "Oh, that's what I was reacting to."

Do you have a strong interest in the science of optics?

I do but it's informal. I like homemade optics, like my eye-glasses. I wear glasses, so I know what happens. I have the feeling that if I explore optics too technically my pictures will lose that folksy quality.

Everything you photograph in this book has both a homely and a homey feeling—the paper bag, the cardboard box, the simplest everyday objects.

That's extremely important to me. I majored in Comparative Religion in college and one of my favorite stories from those studies is about Meister Eckhart, the Christian mystic. The Church didn't like him much because he felt one could talk directly to God. One of his lines was something like, "You go in the woods, you break a stick, and there is Jesus." Magic is around the corner. Minor White's best work gave me that sense too. In the weird light of some of his pictures sometimes you can see a piece of a real room that you feel you can enter.

What are you up to now?

I haven't taken a good picture of my daughter, Laura, yet and she's almost four. I'm also interested in doing some pictures of simple science experiments. And I want to do pictures of words—like Latin printed with woodblocks. I want to find a way to show that language is something partly physical. I don't know how to do that yet, but I'm working on it.

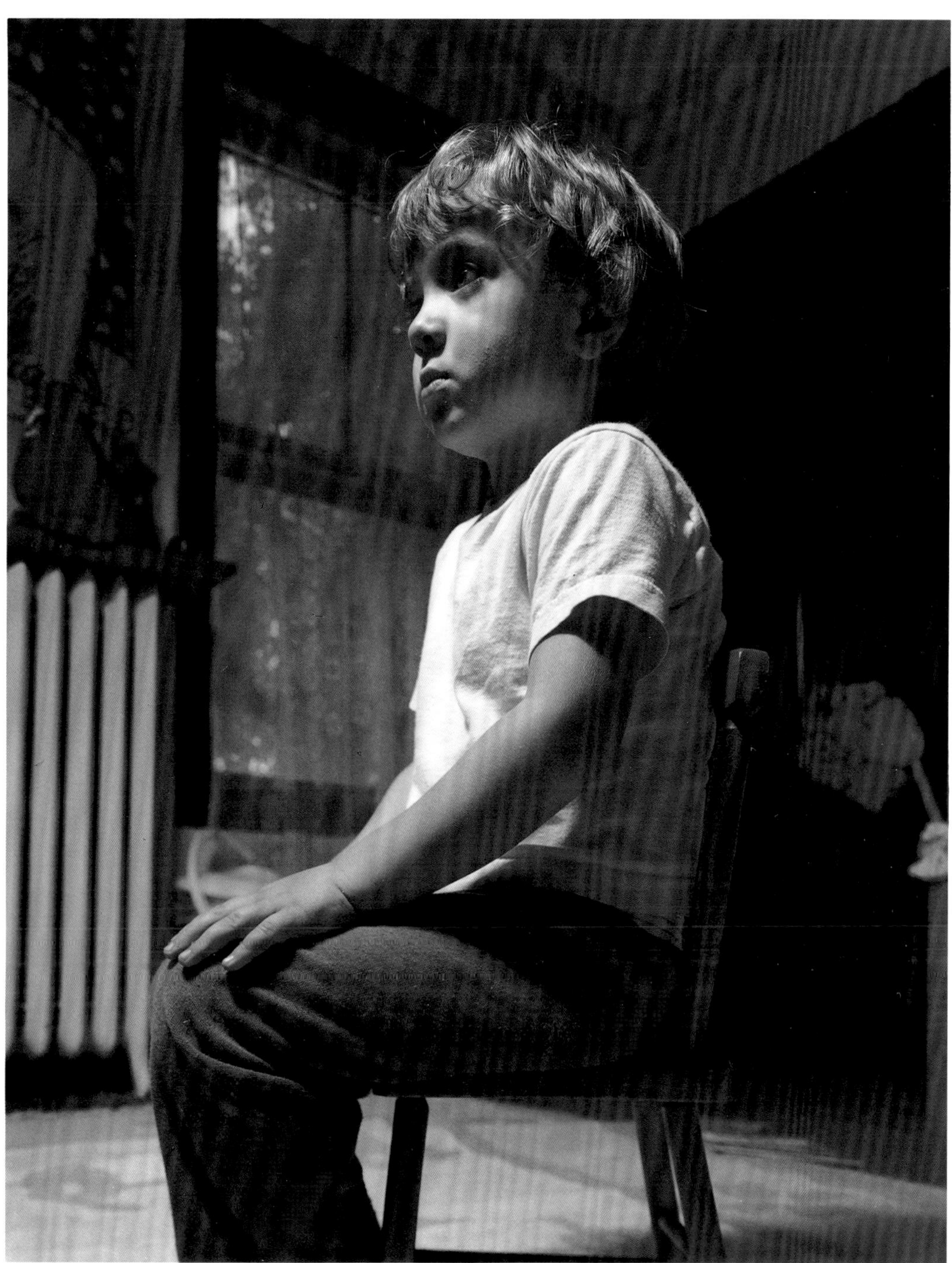

Brady Sitting, 1989

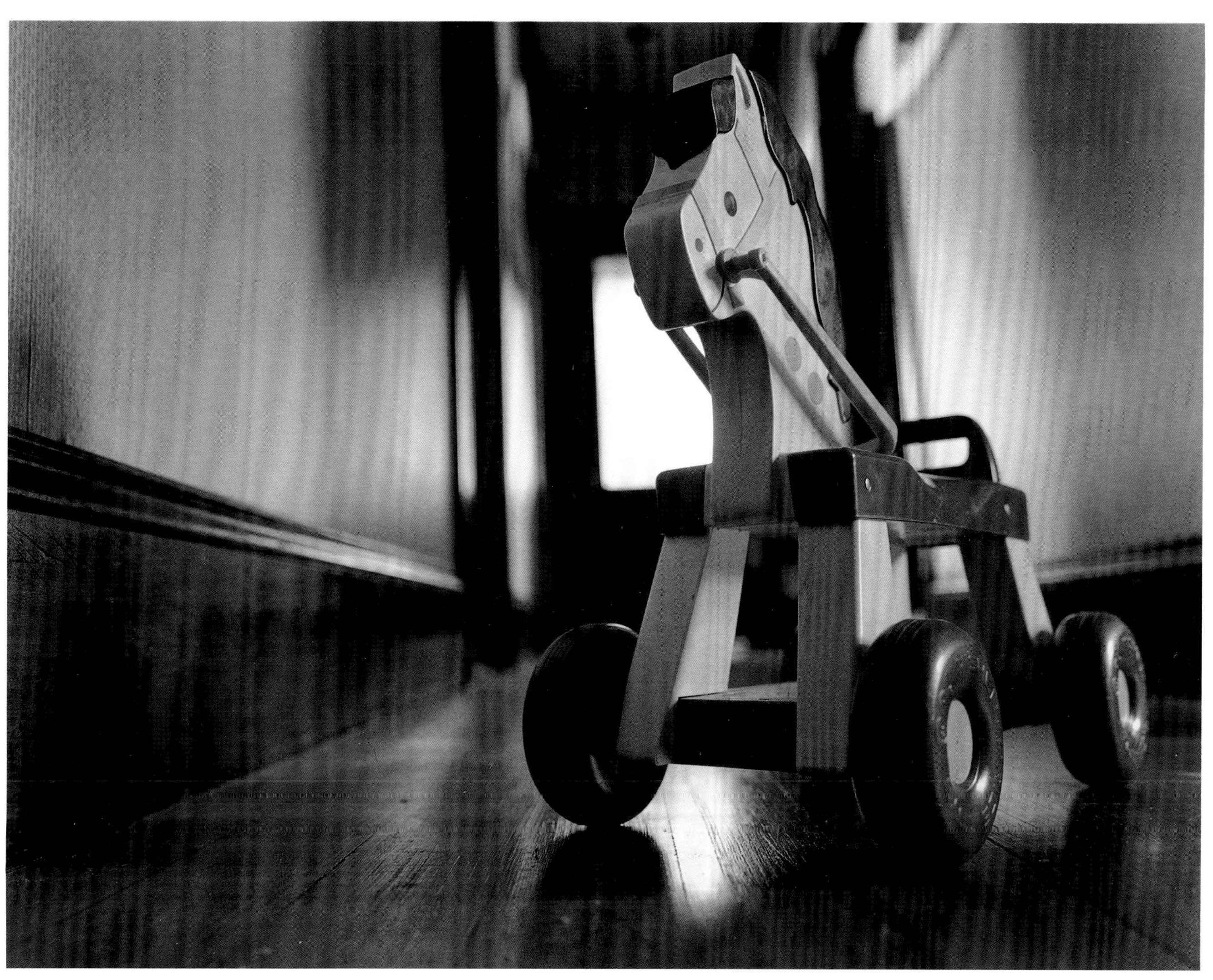

Toy Horse, 1987

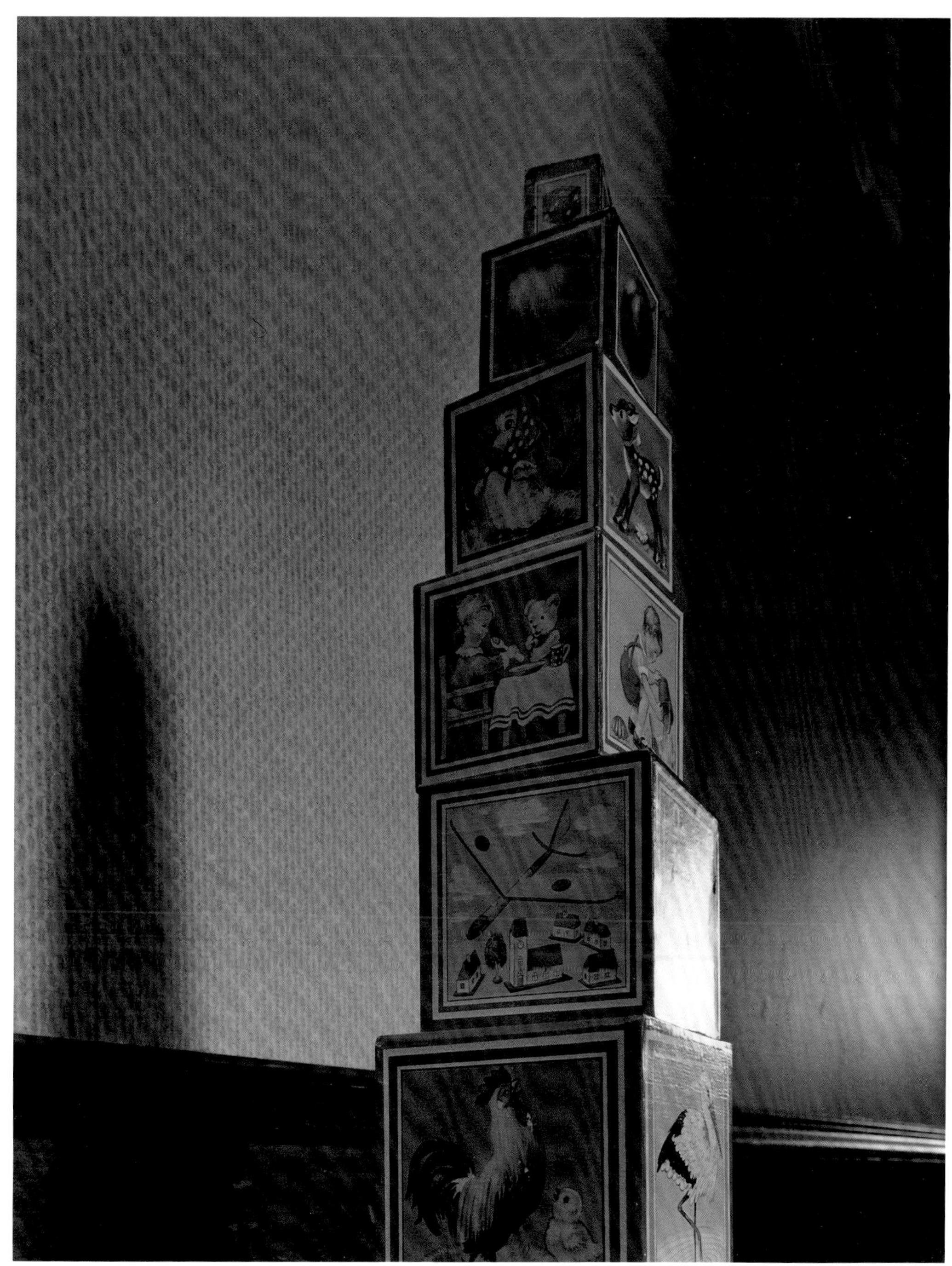

Toy Blocks, 1987

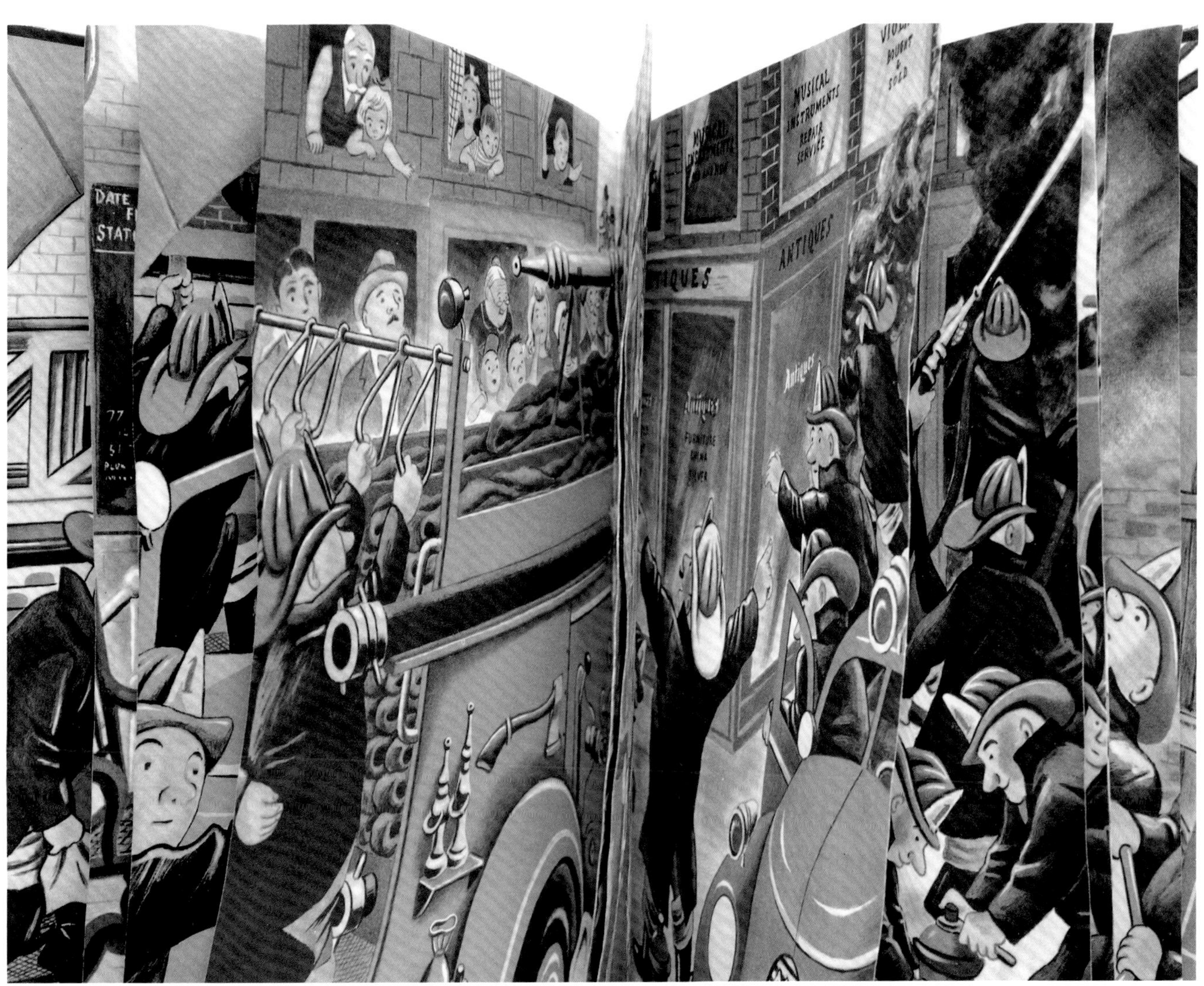

Children's Book, 1987

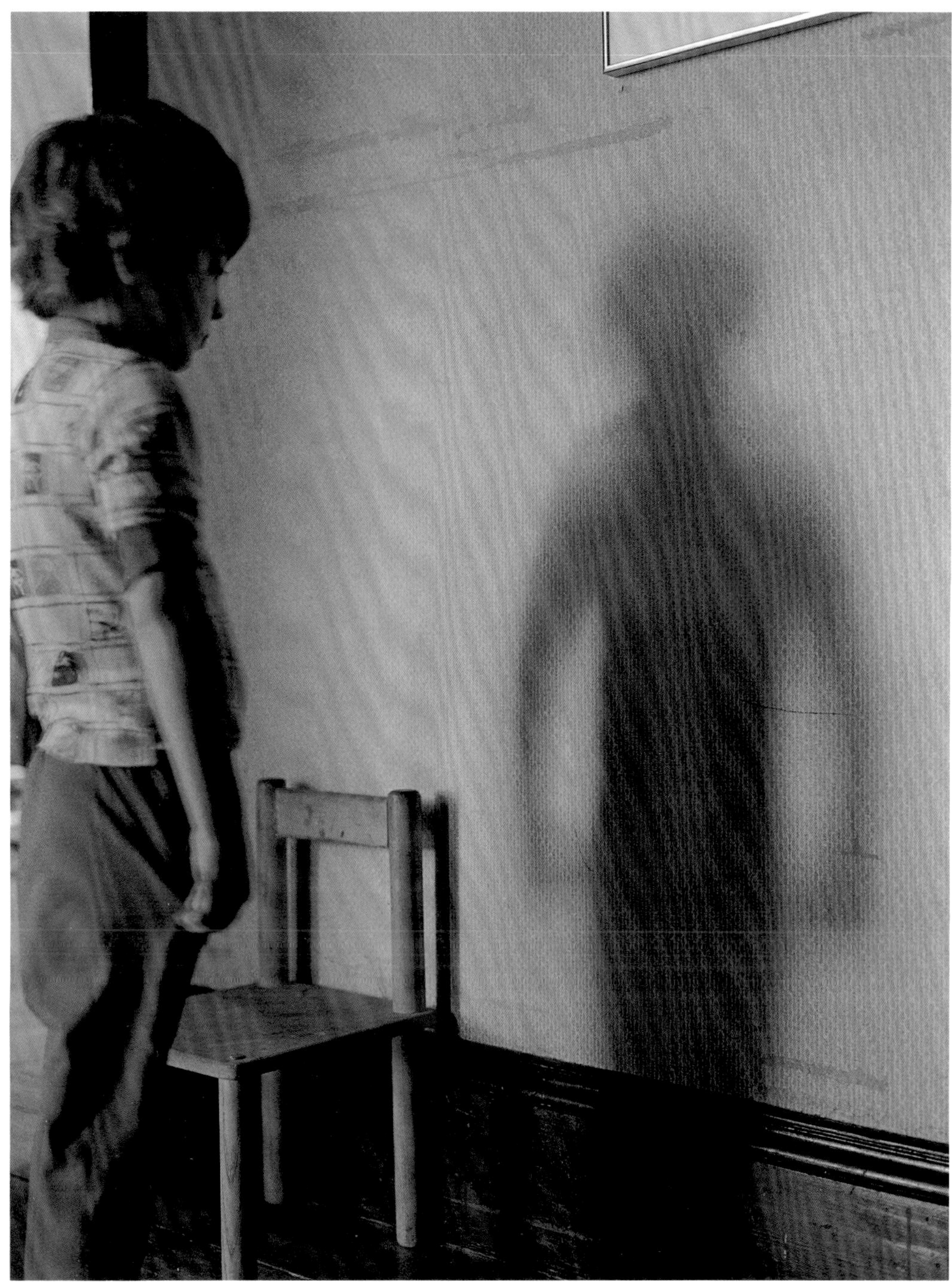

Brady Looking at His Shadow, 1990

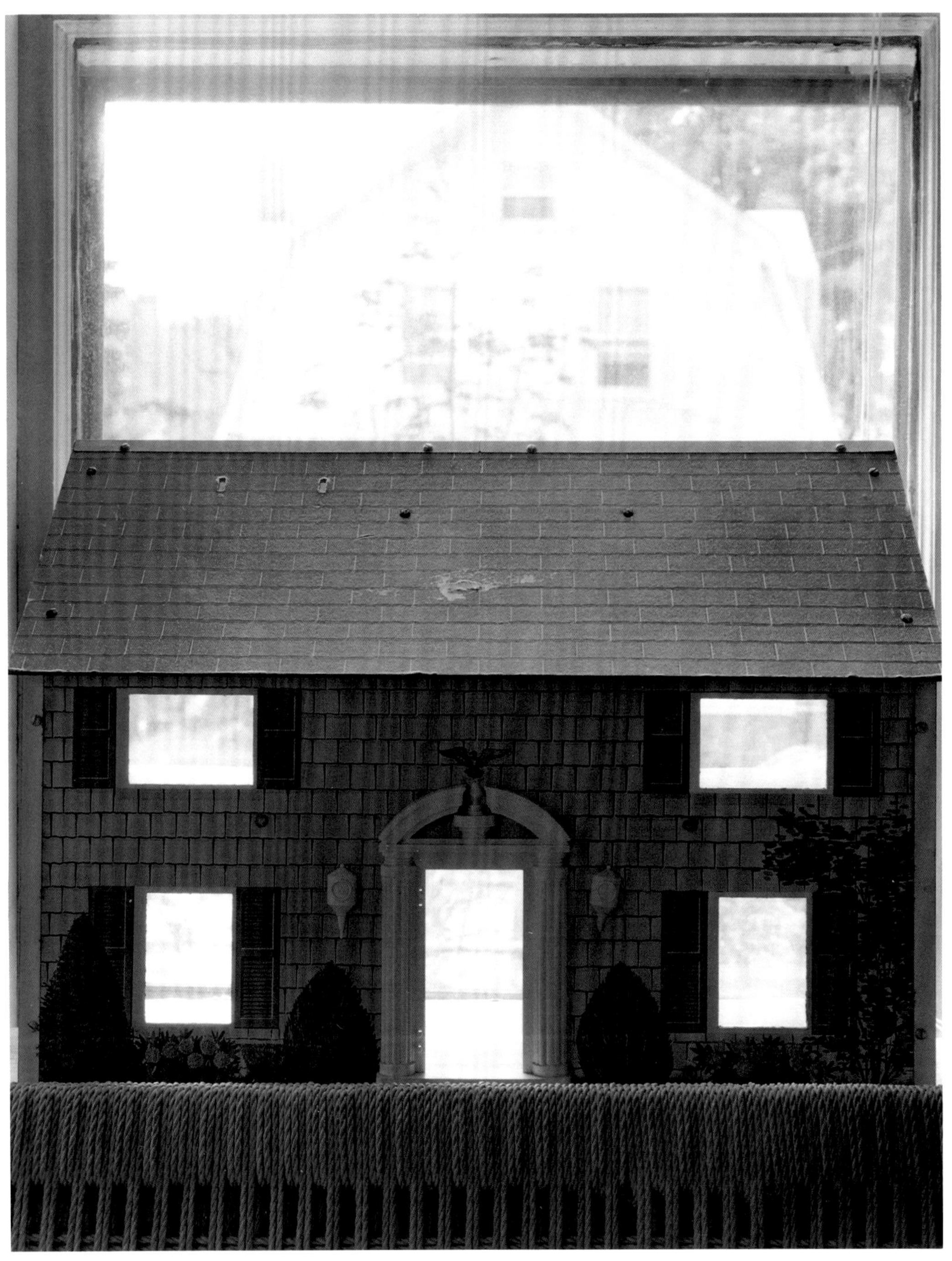

Doll House, 1987

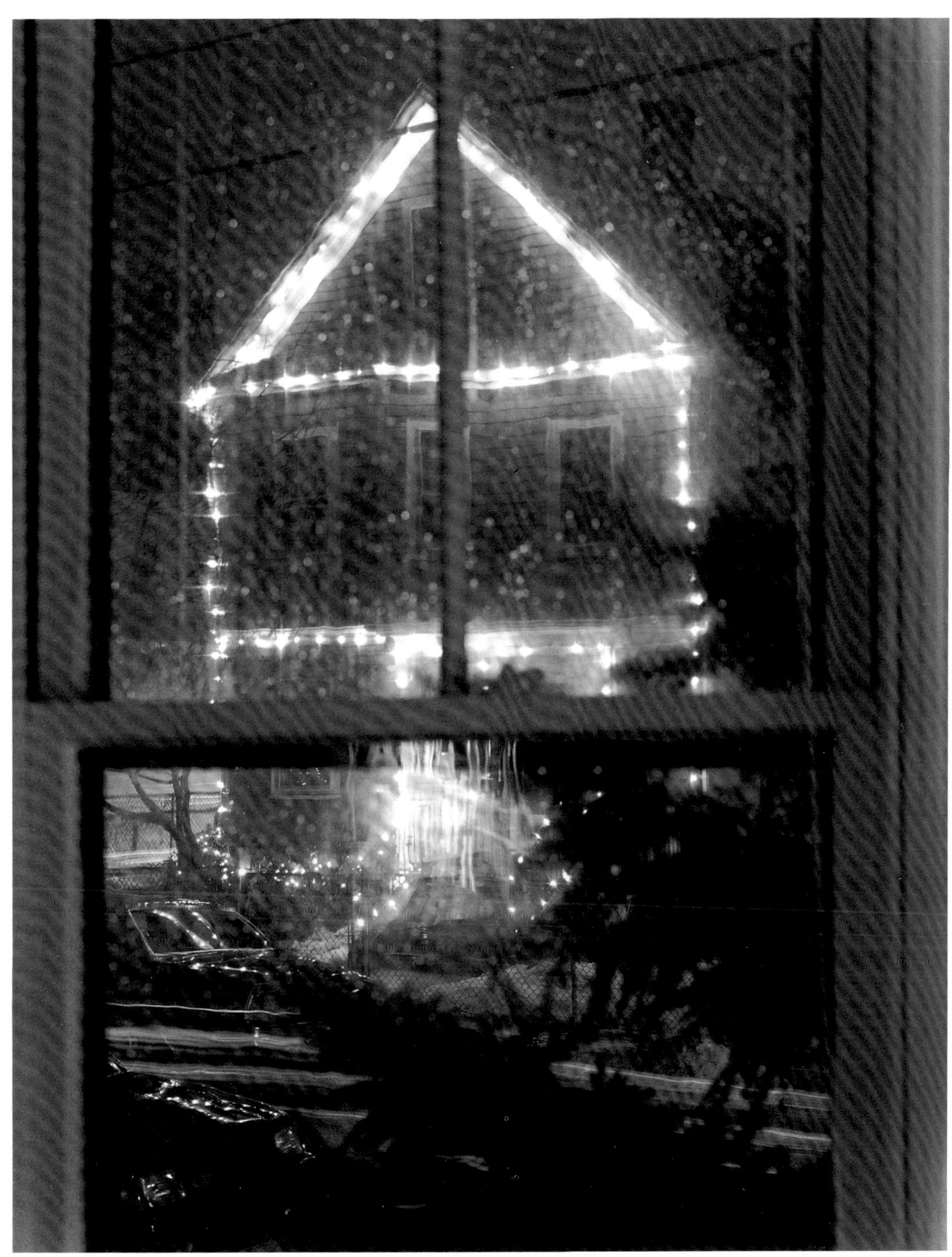

New Year's Eve, 1989–90

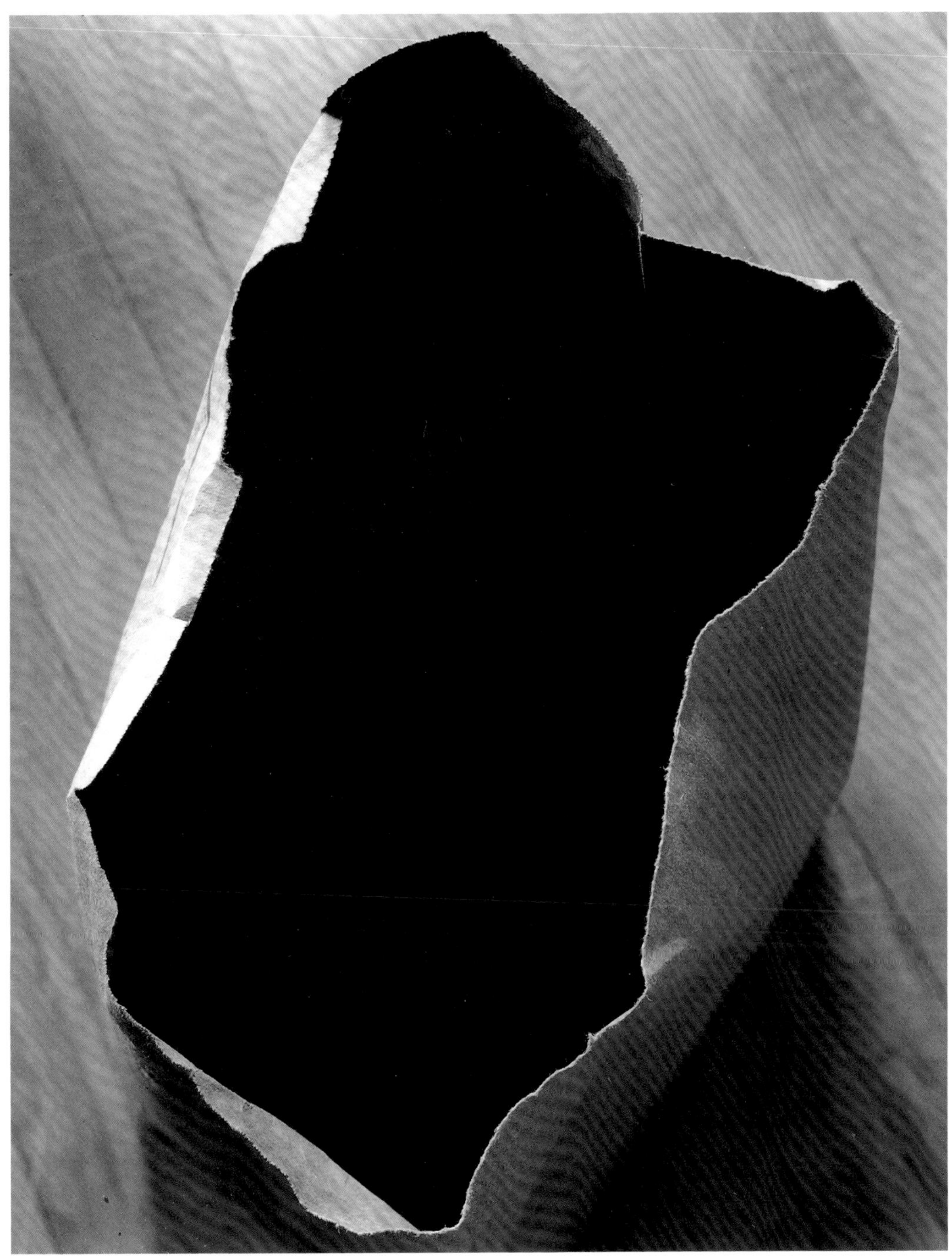

Paper Bag, 1992

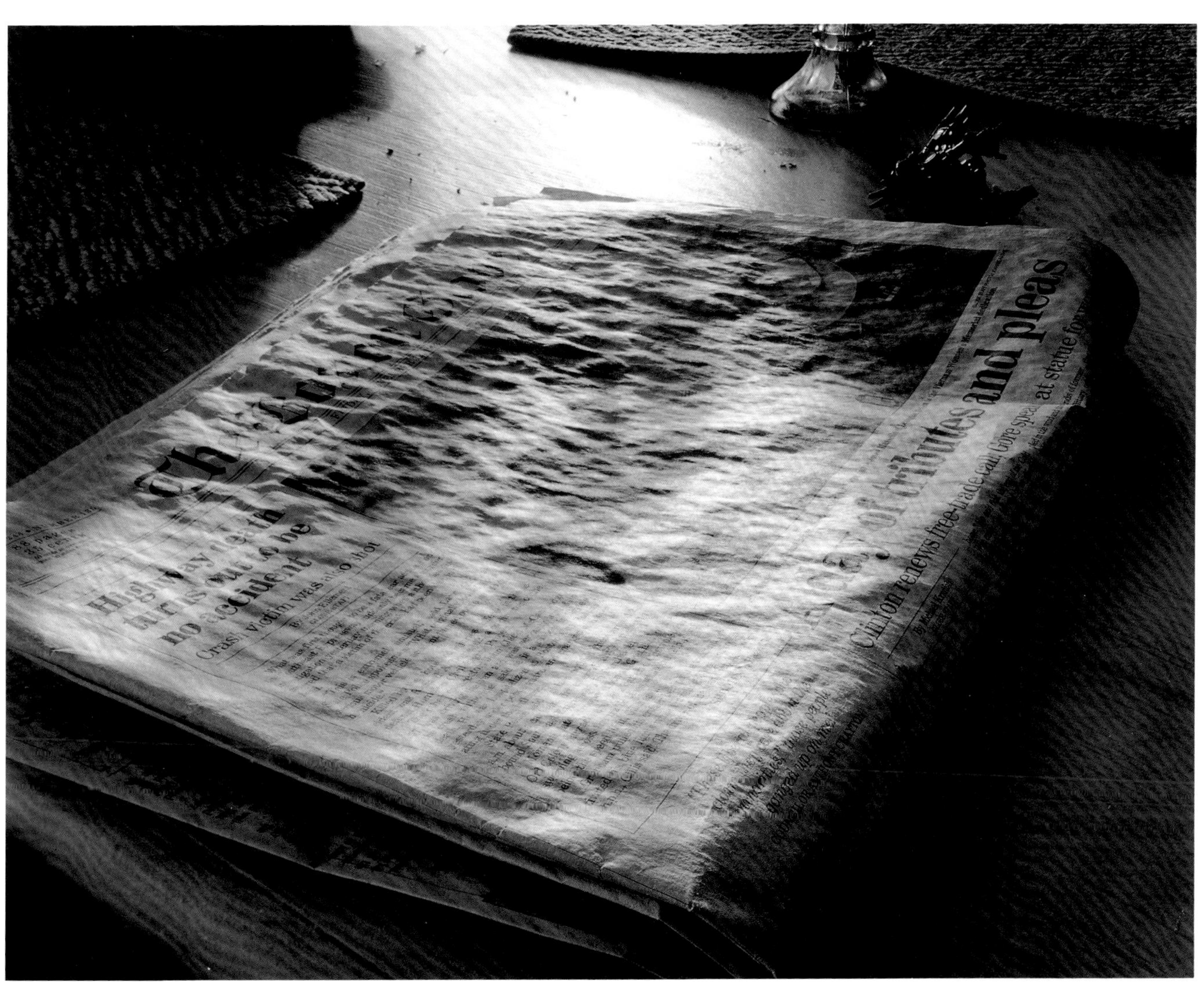

Newspaper, 1993

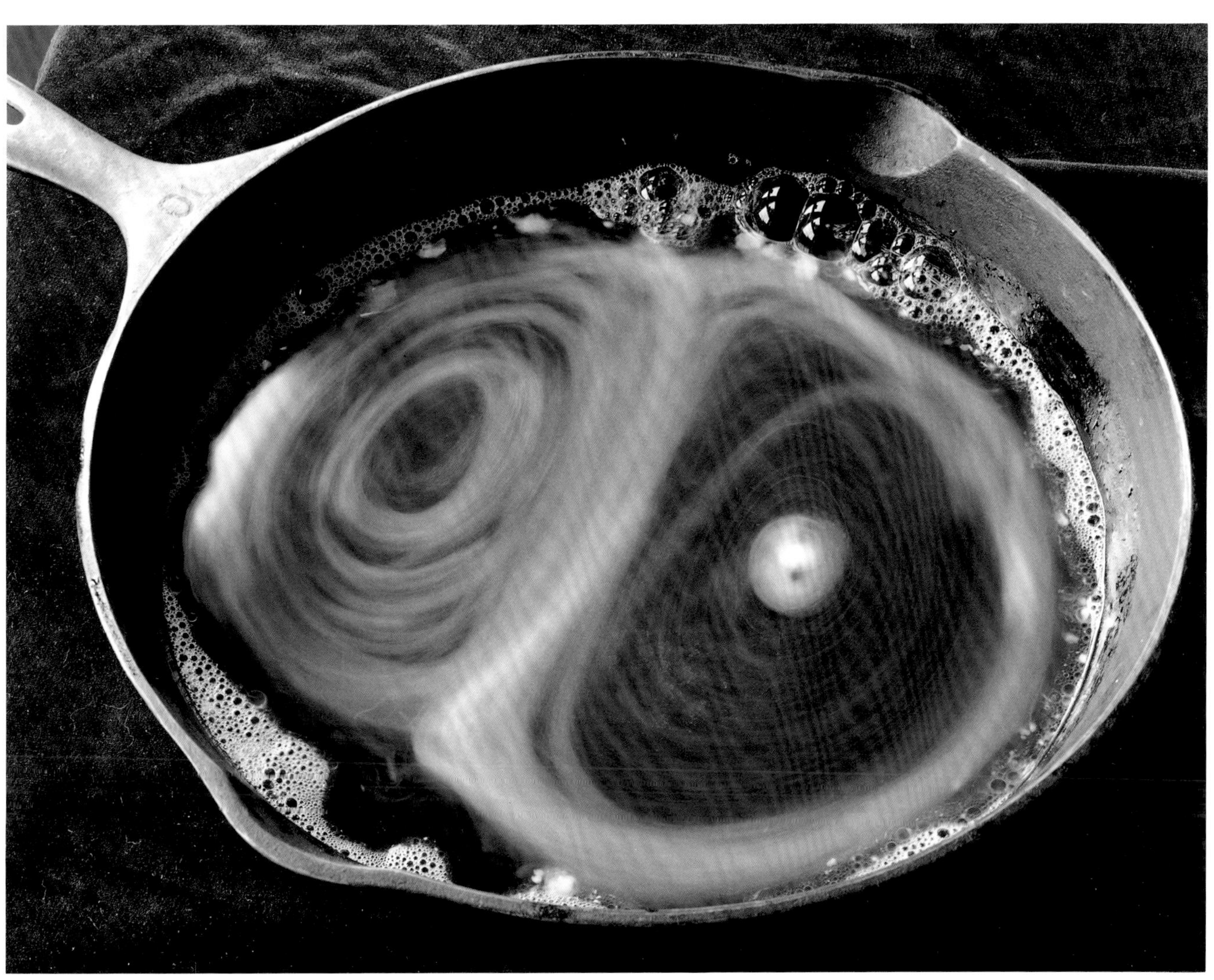

Motion of Soapy Water in Pan, 1994

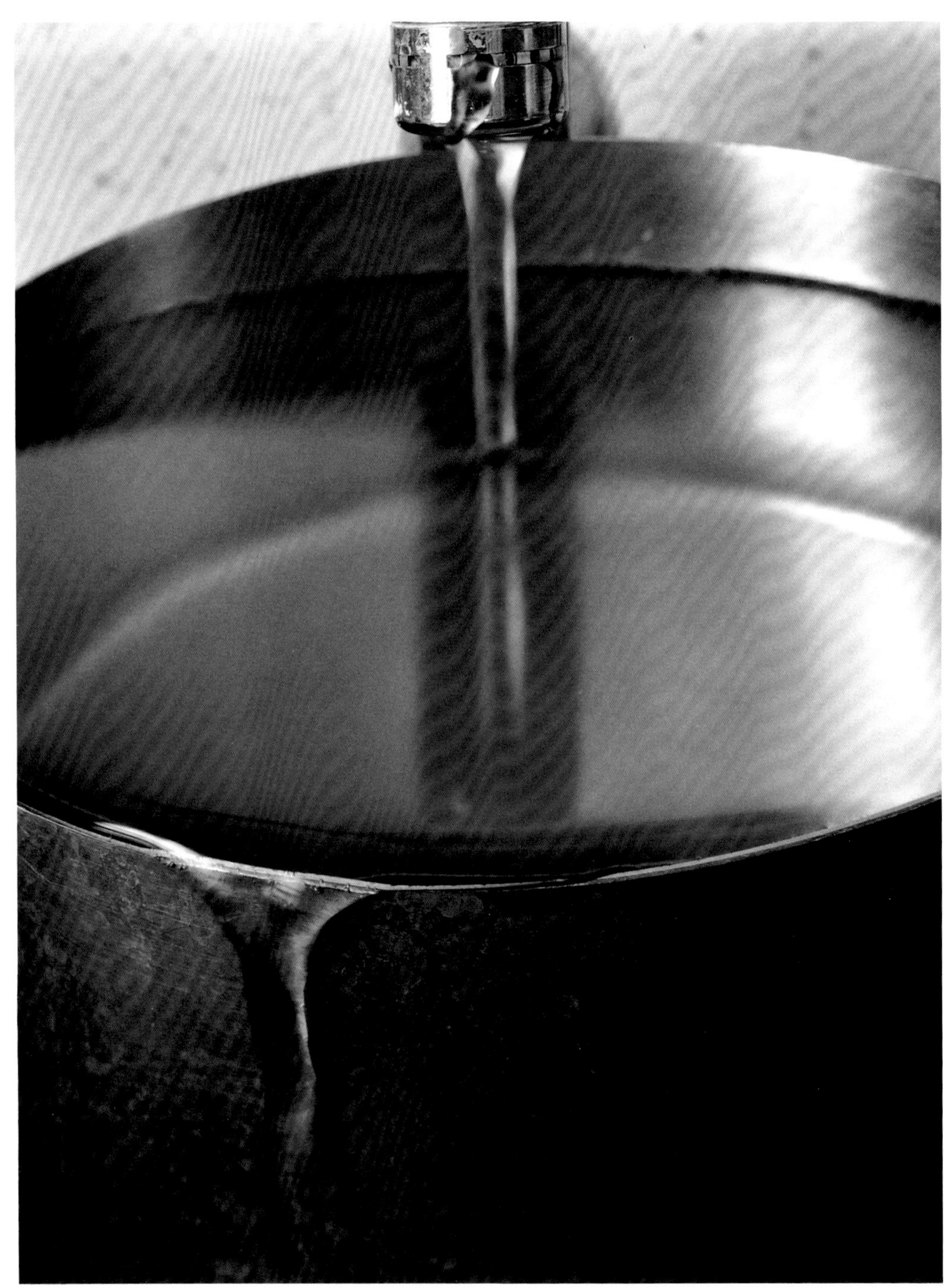

Running Water, 1993

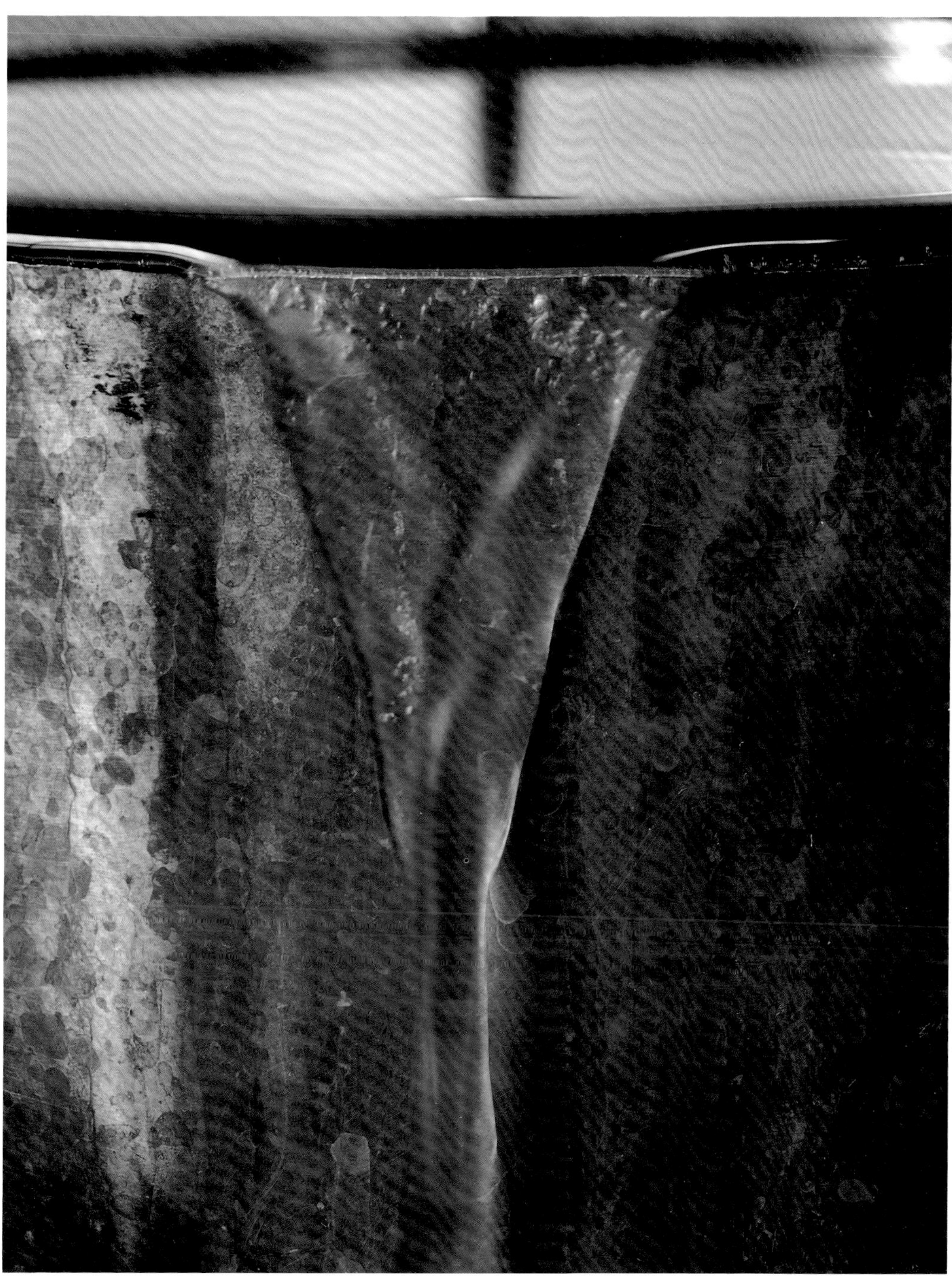

Water Pouring Out of a Pot, 1993

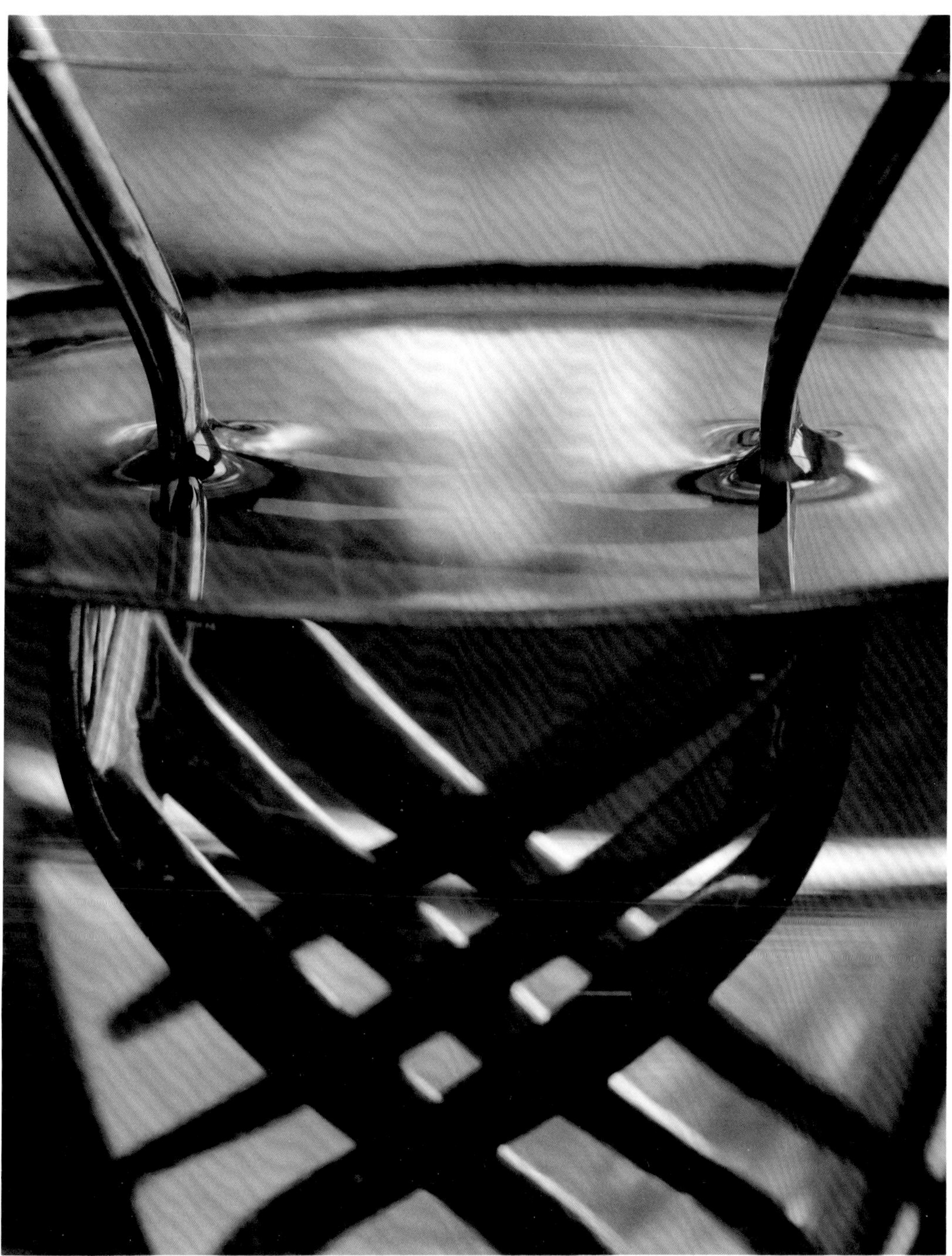

Two Forks Under Water, 1993

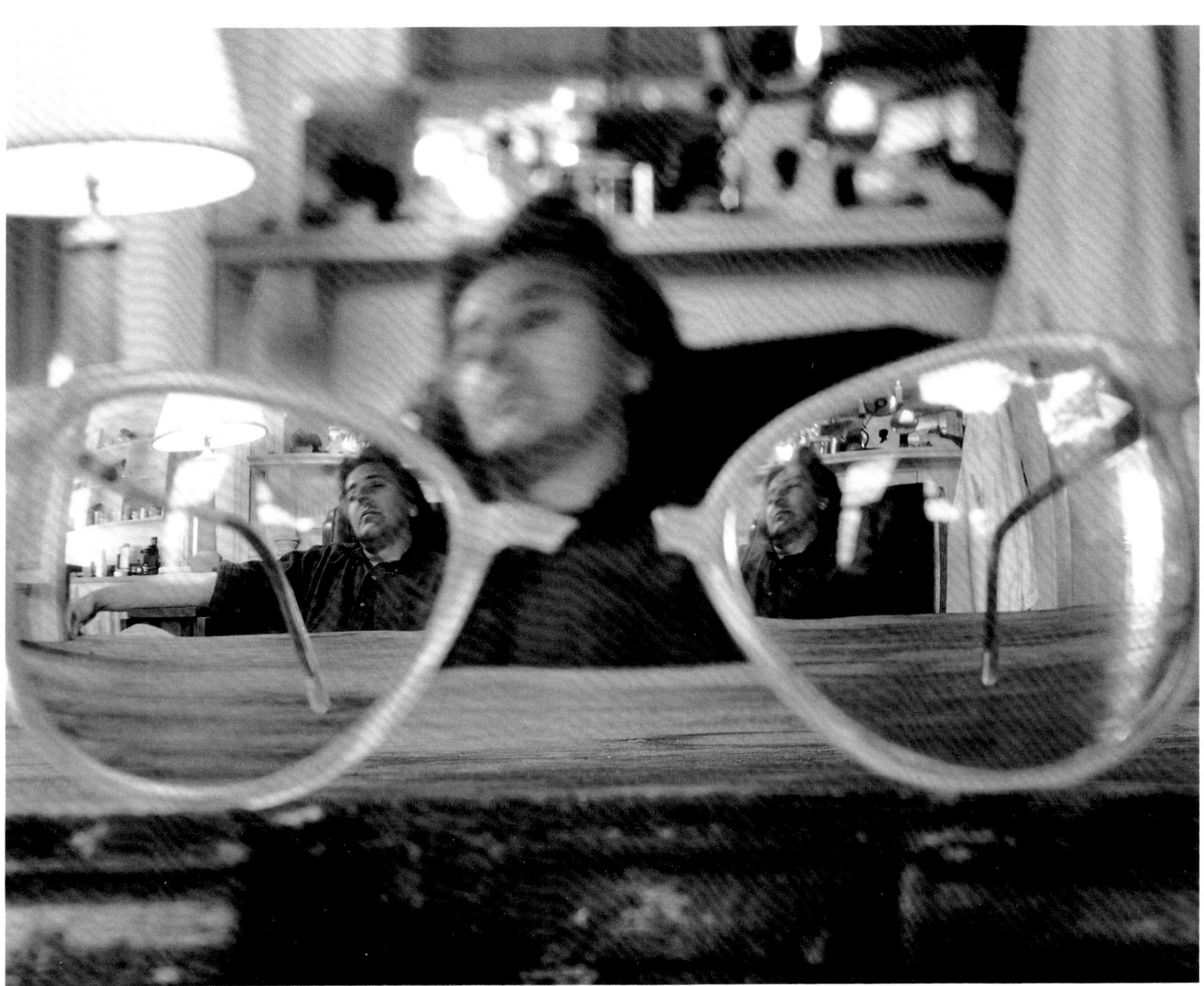

My Broken Glasses and Me, 1994

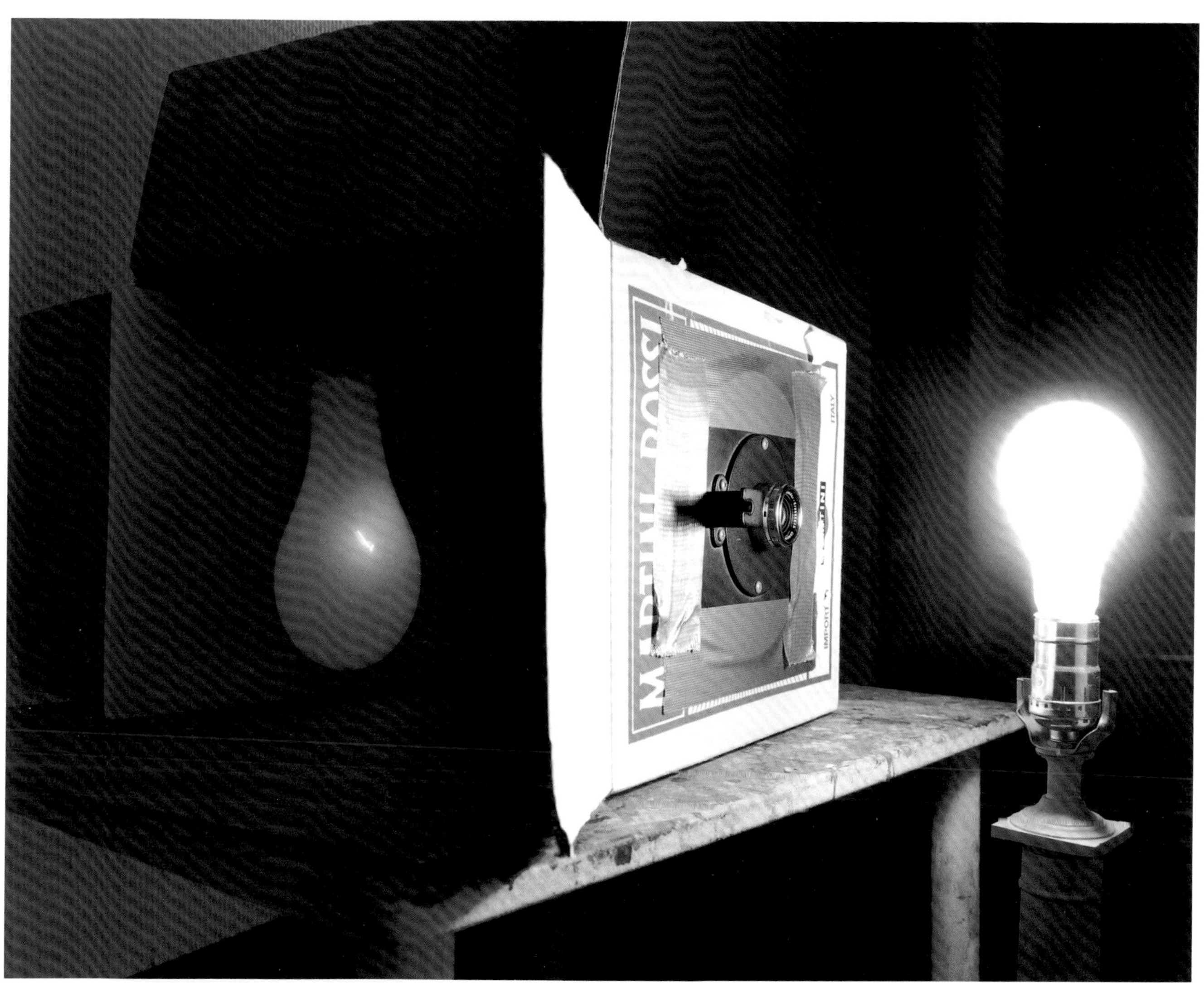

Light Bulb, 1991

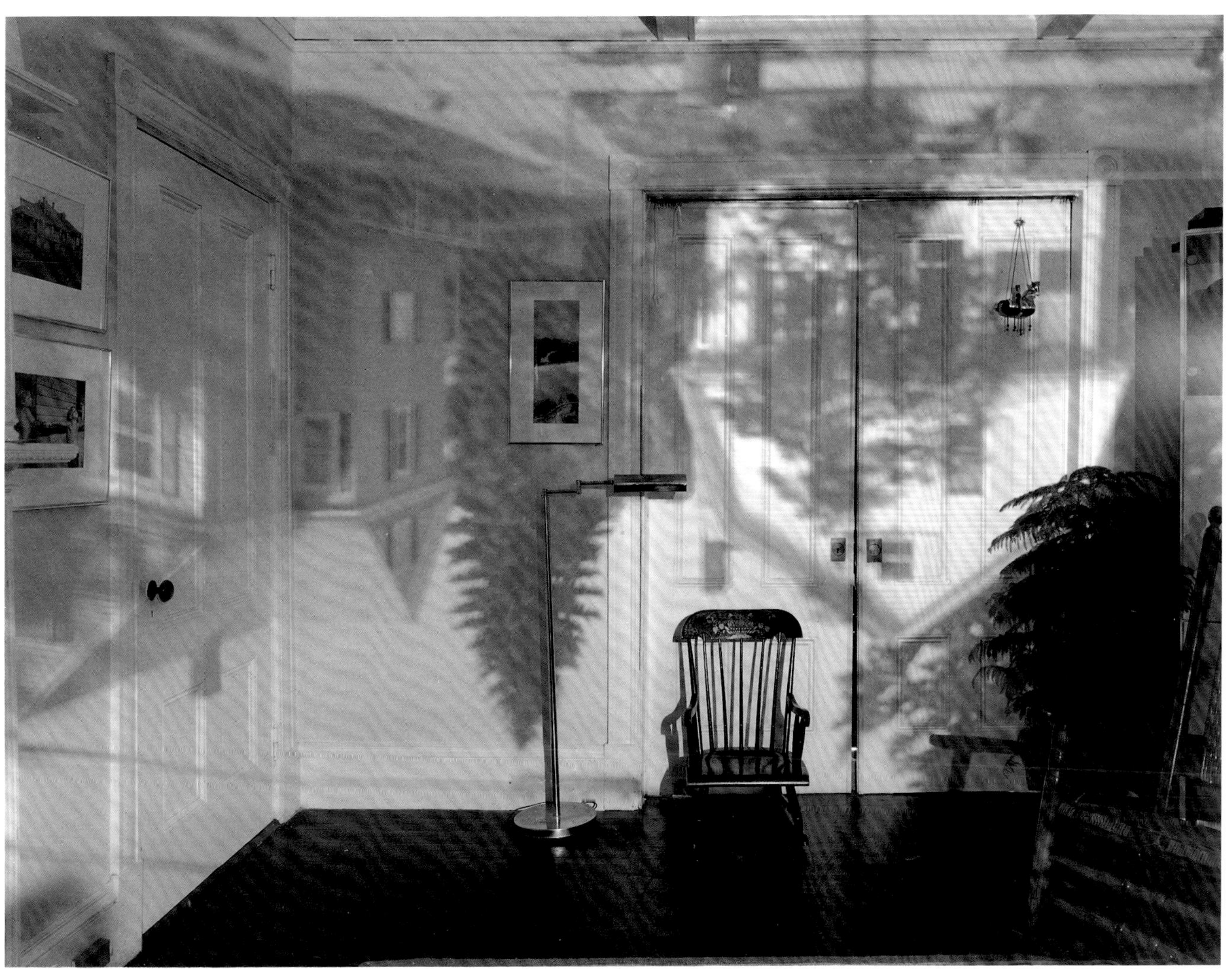

Camera Obscura Image of Houses Across the Street in Our Livingroom, 1991

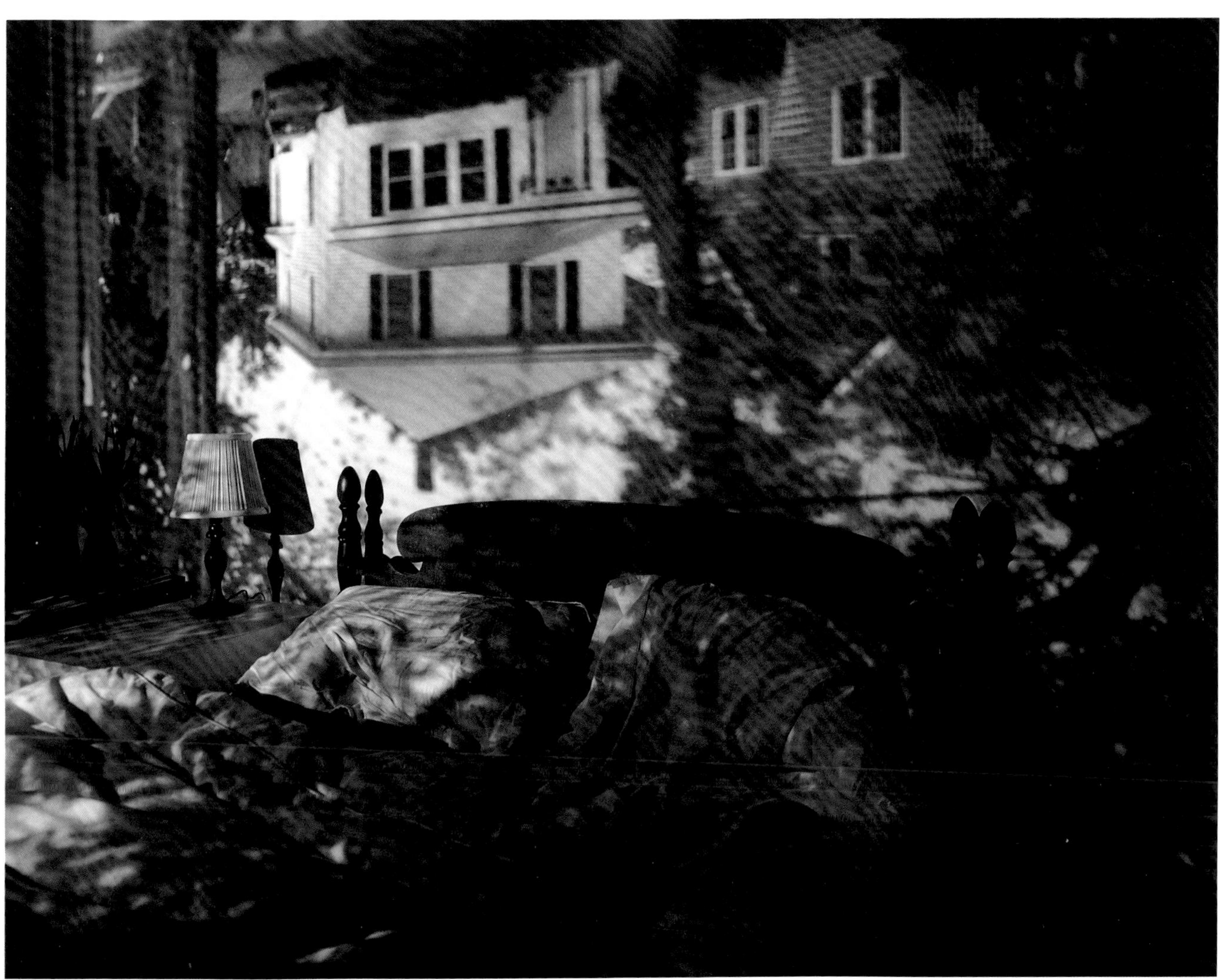

Camera Obscura Image of Houses Across the Street in Our Bedroom, 1991

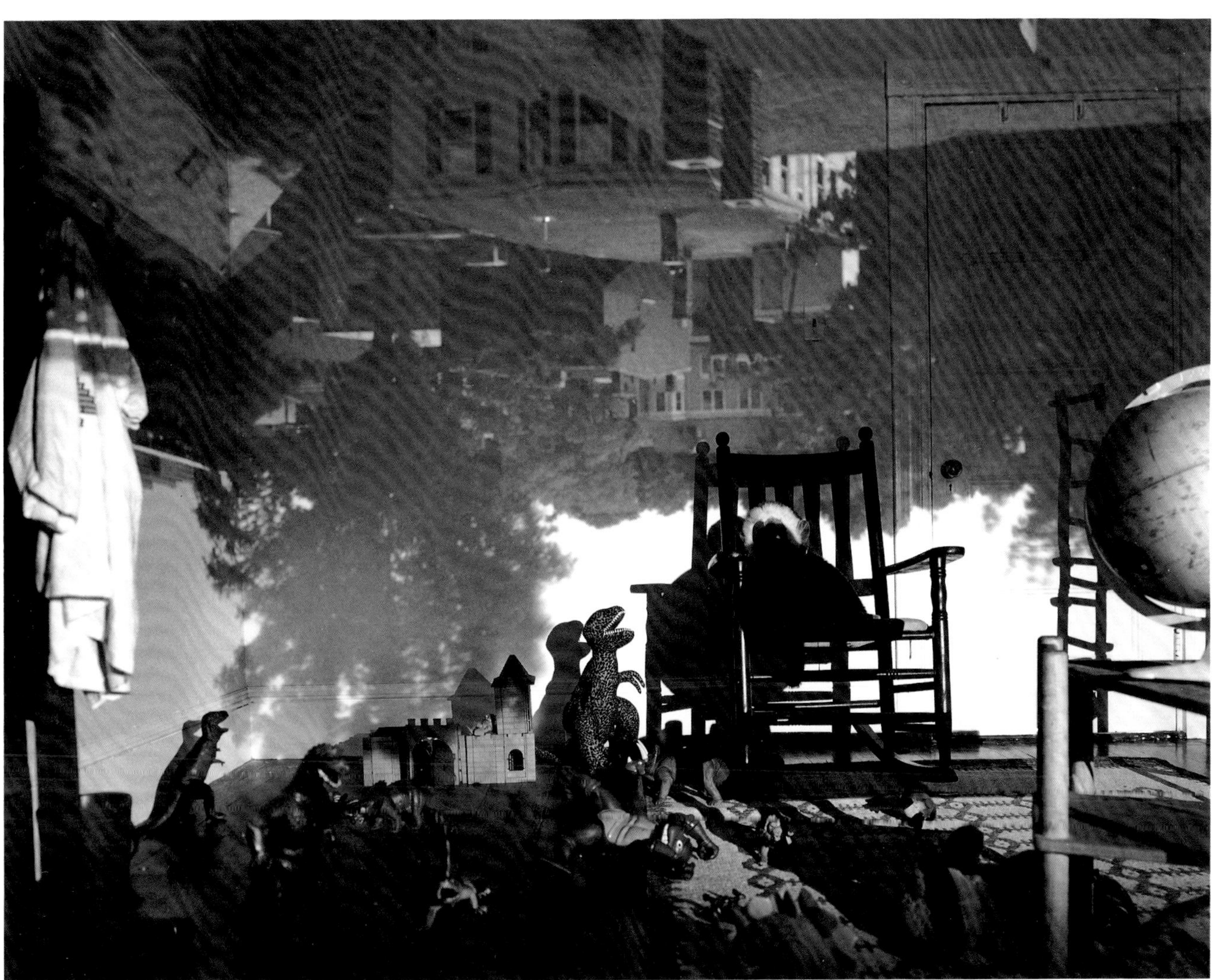

Camera Obscura Image of Brookline View in Brady's Room, 1992

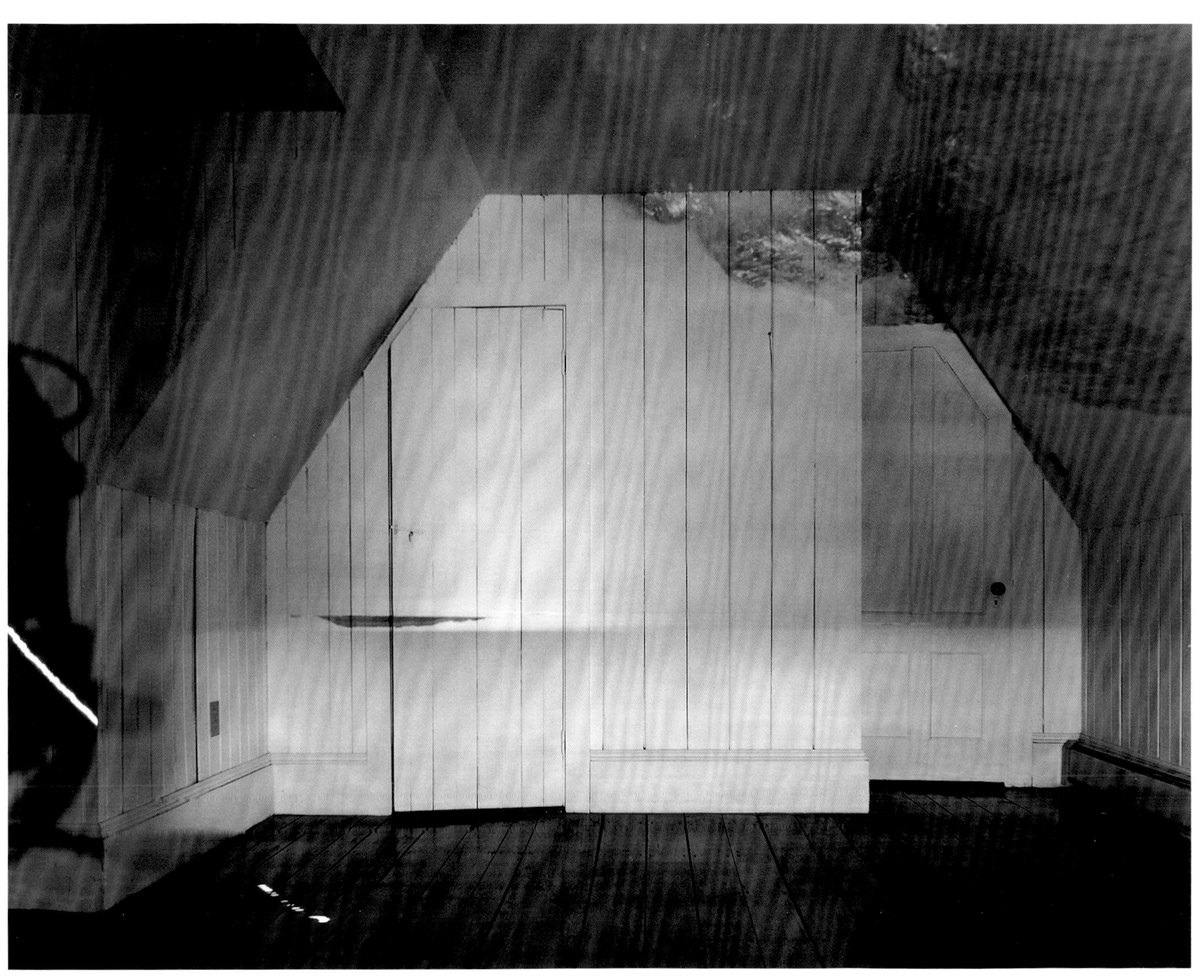

Camera Obscura Image of the Sea in Attic, 1994

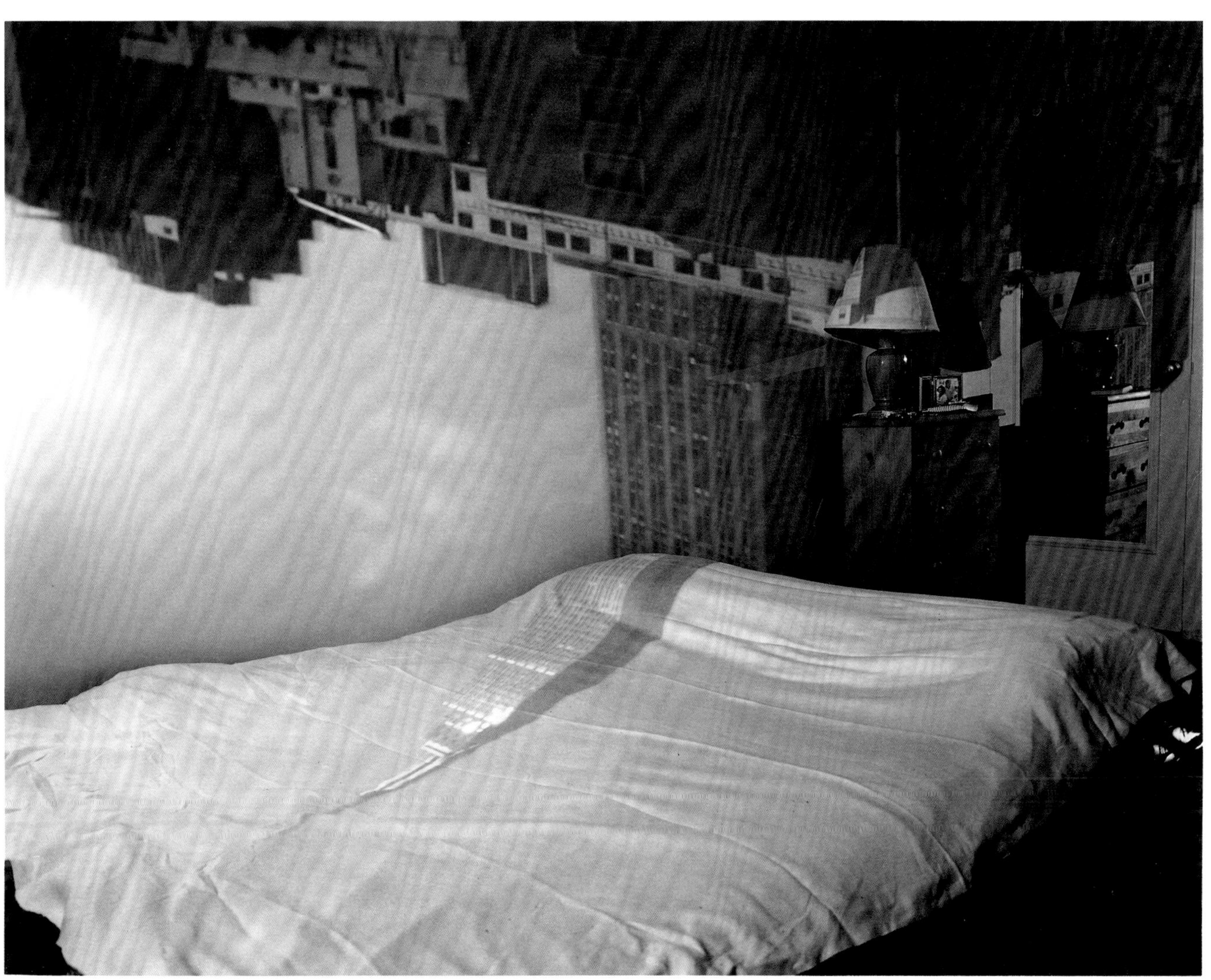

Camera Obscura Image of the Empire State Building in Bedroom, 1994

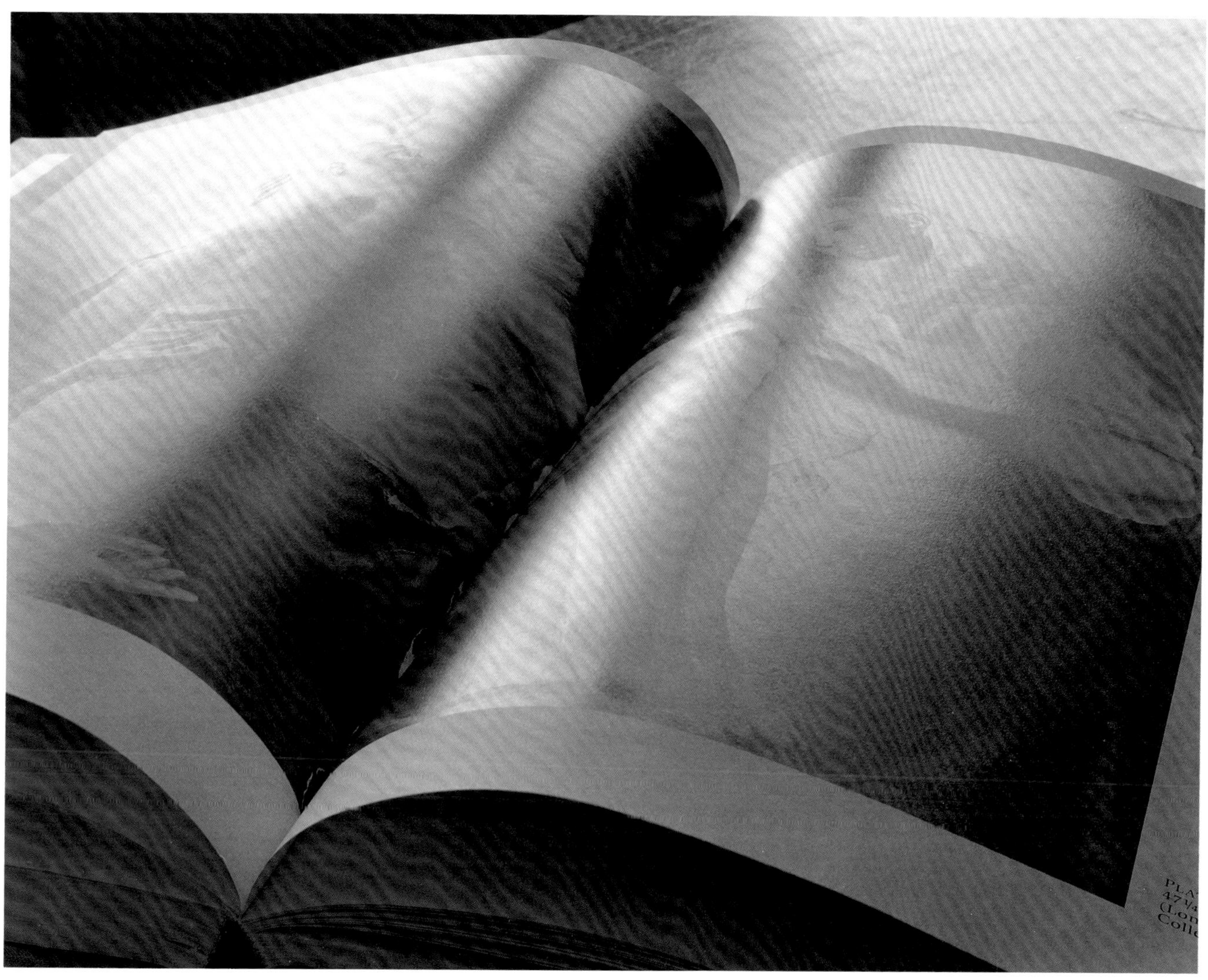

Book: *Pietà* by El Greco, 1993

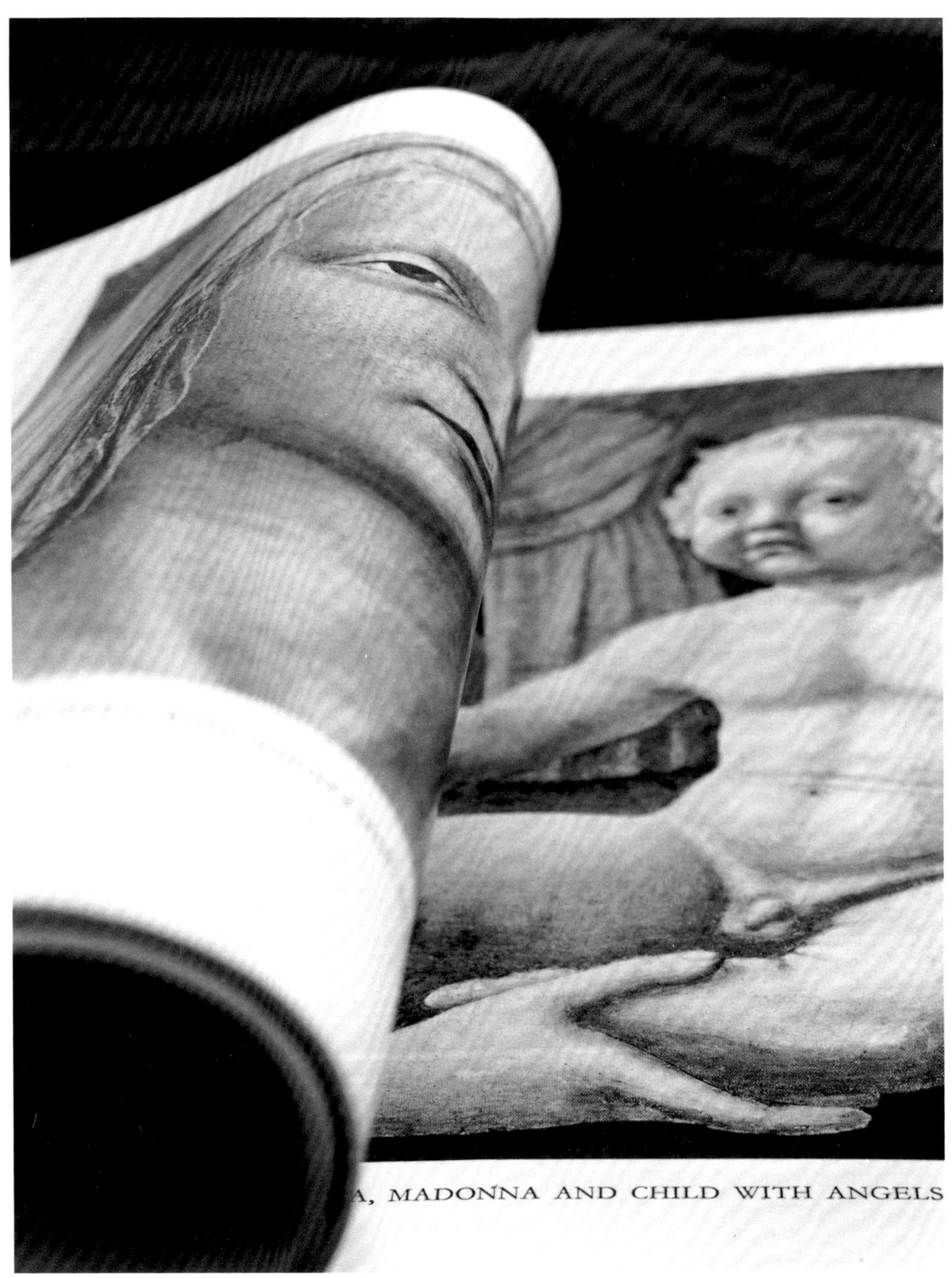

Book: Detail from *Saint Anna, Madonna and Child with Angels* by Masaccio, 1993

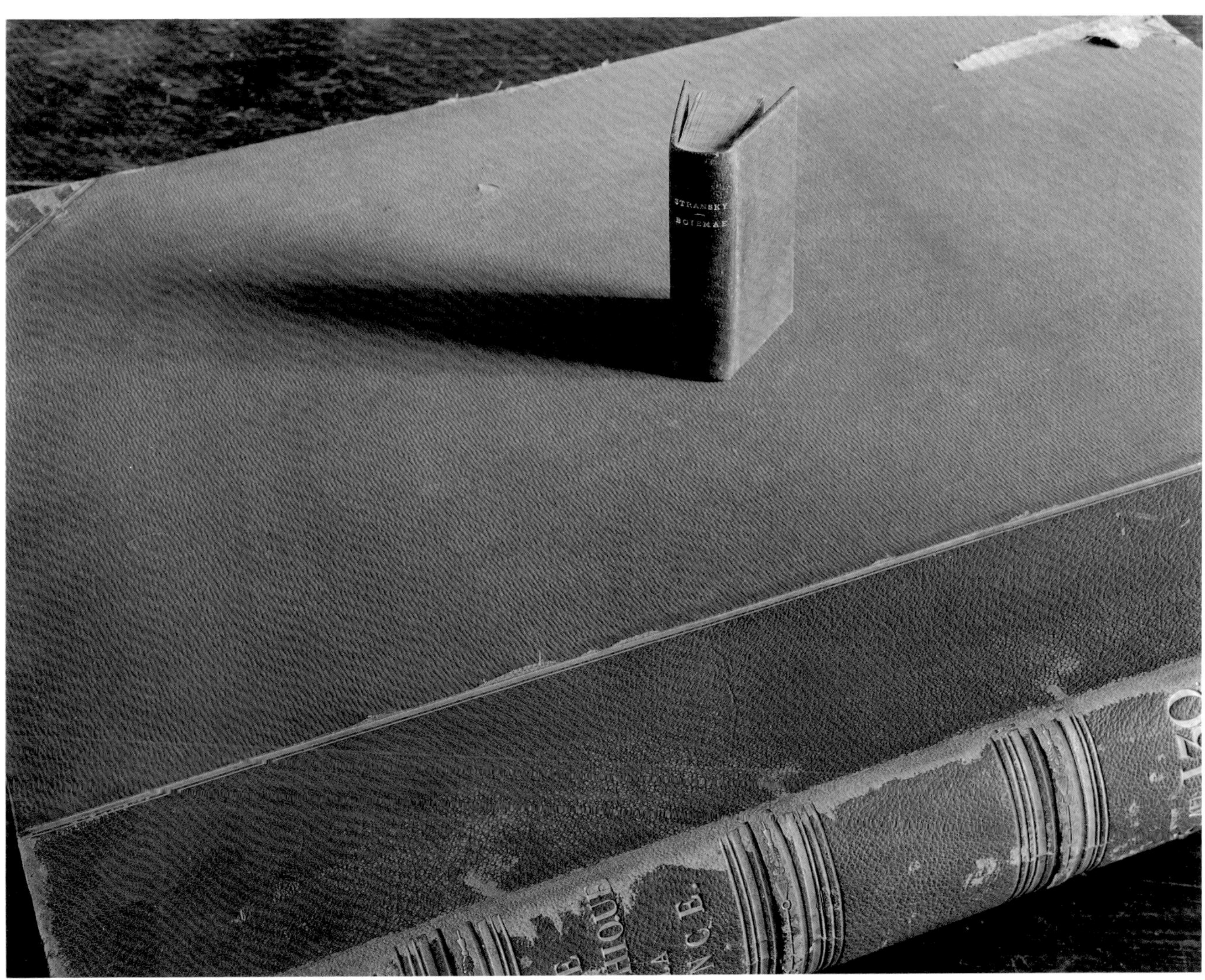

Two Books, 1994

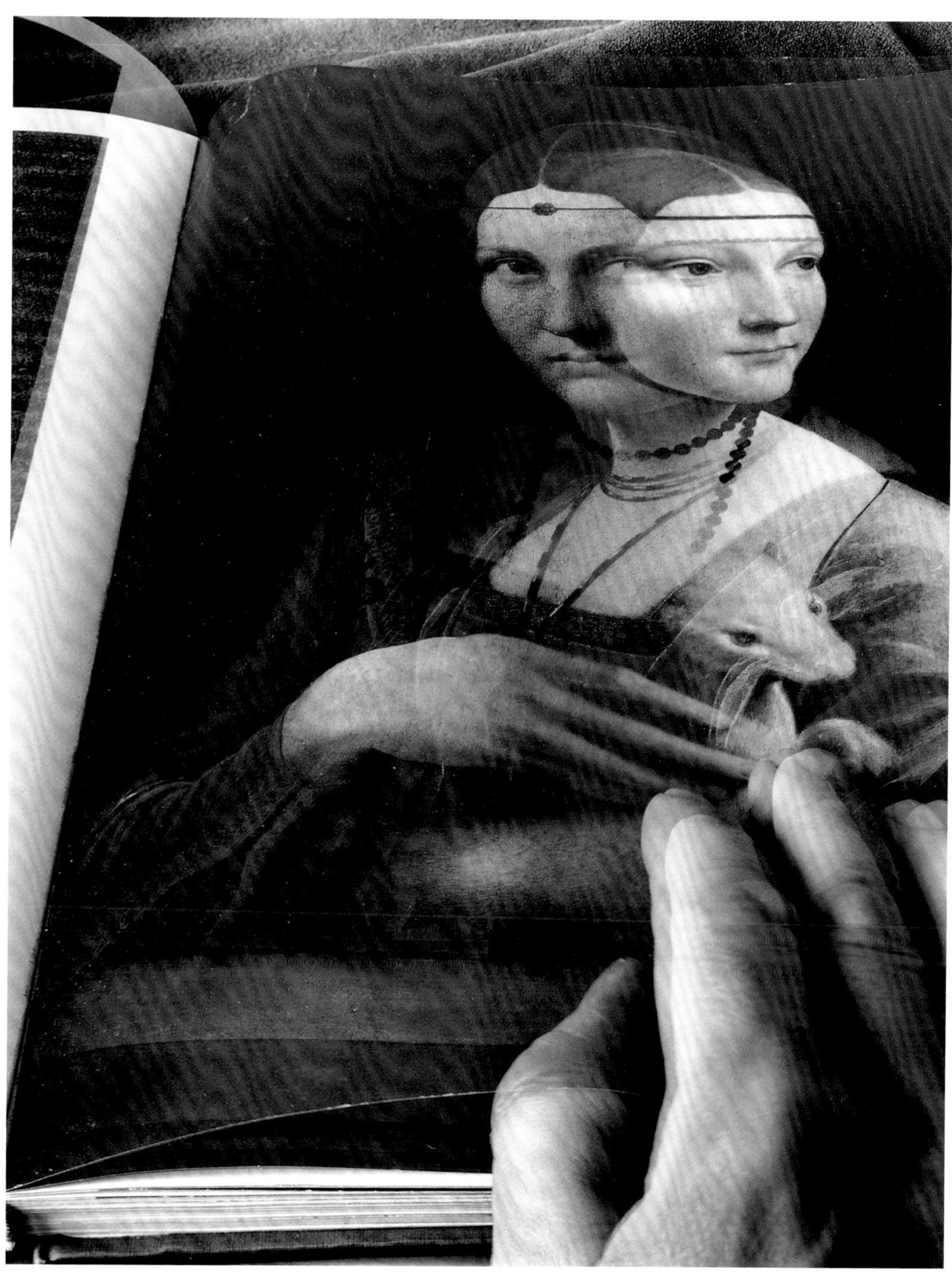

Book: Portraits by Da Vinci and School of Da Vinci, 1993

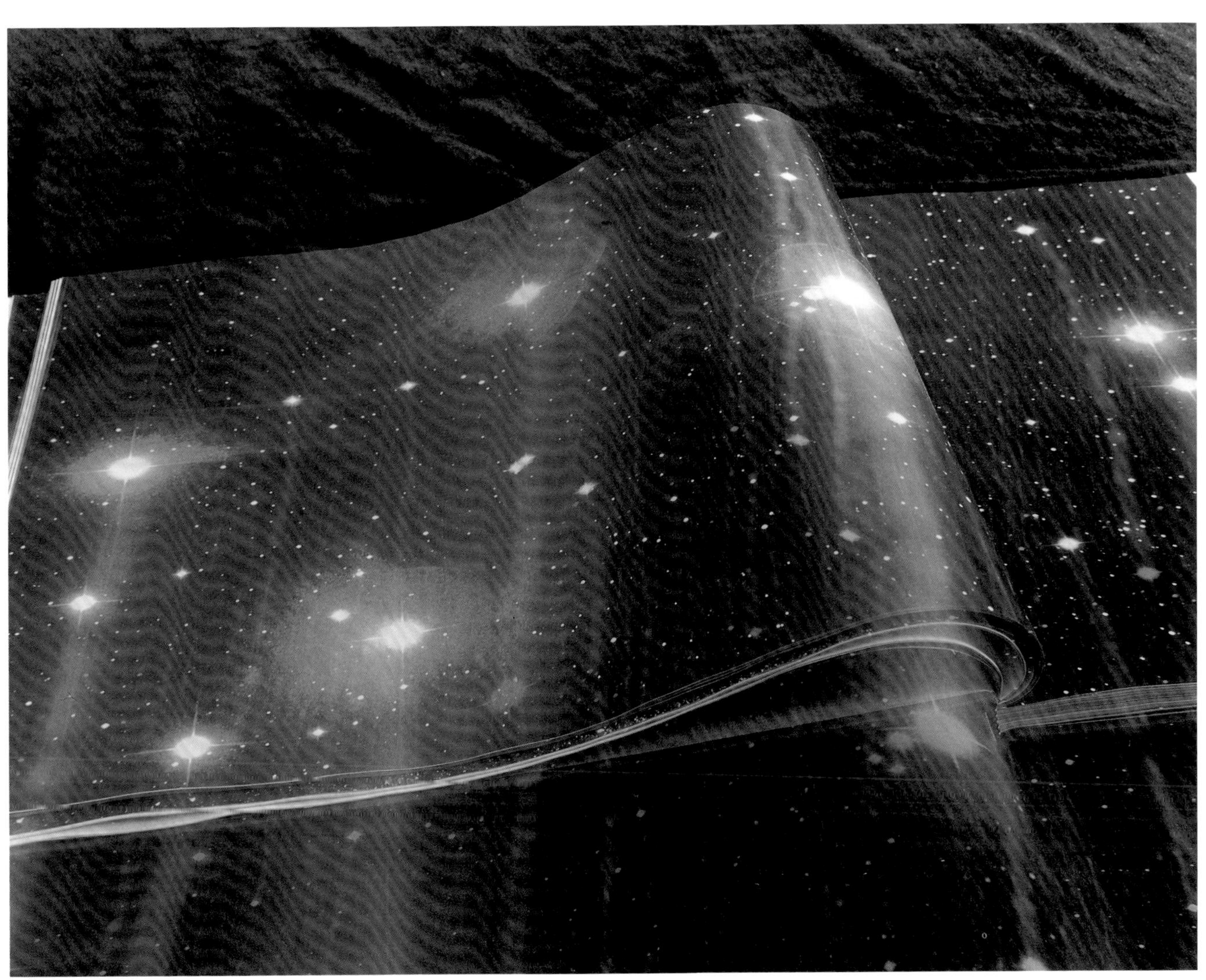

Book of Stars, 1994

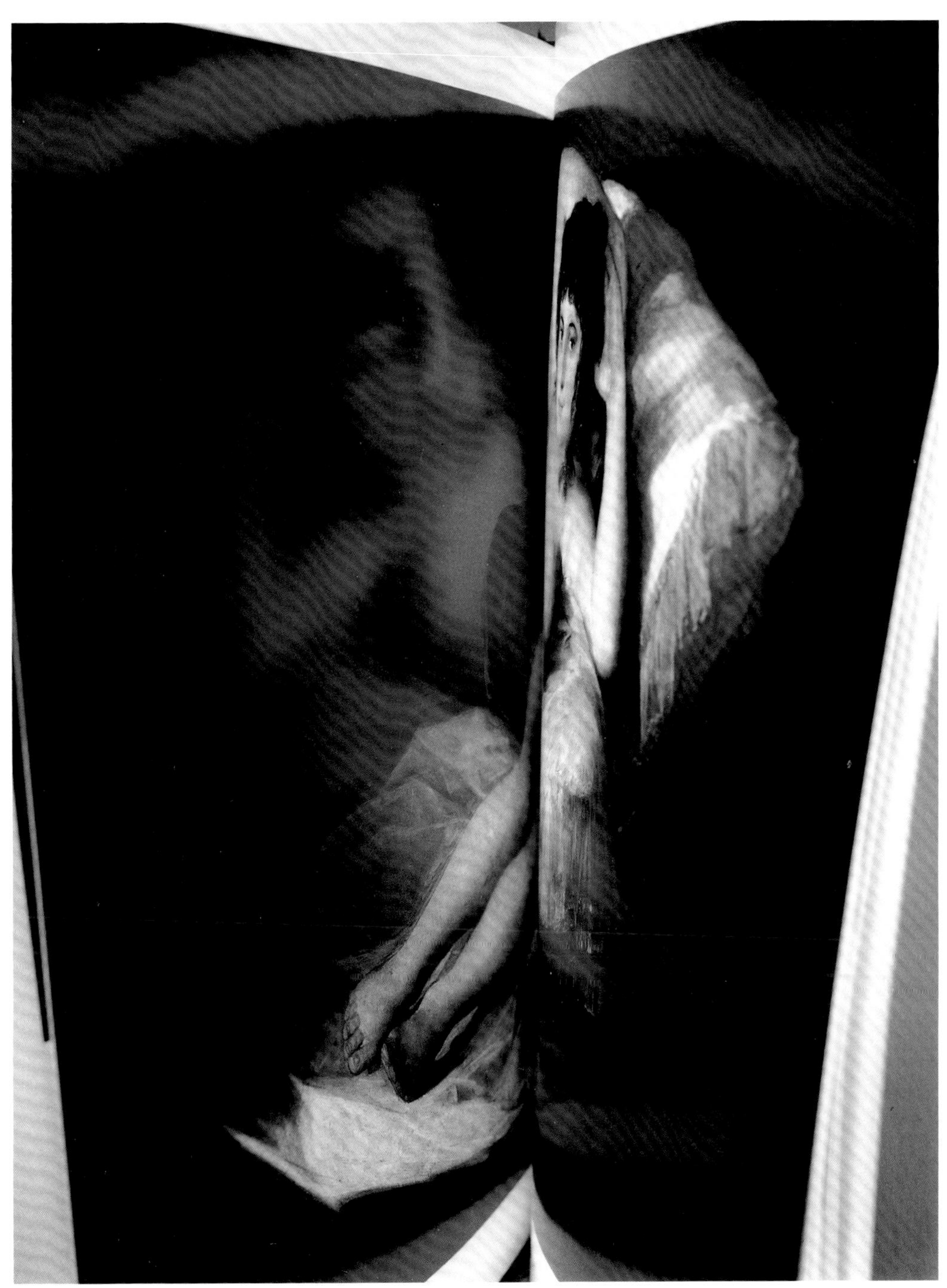

Book: *The Naked Maja* by Goya, 1994

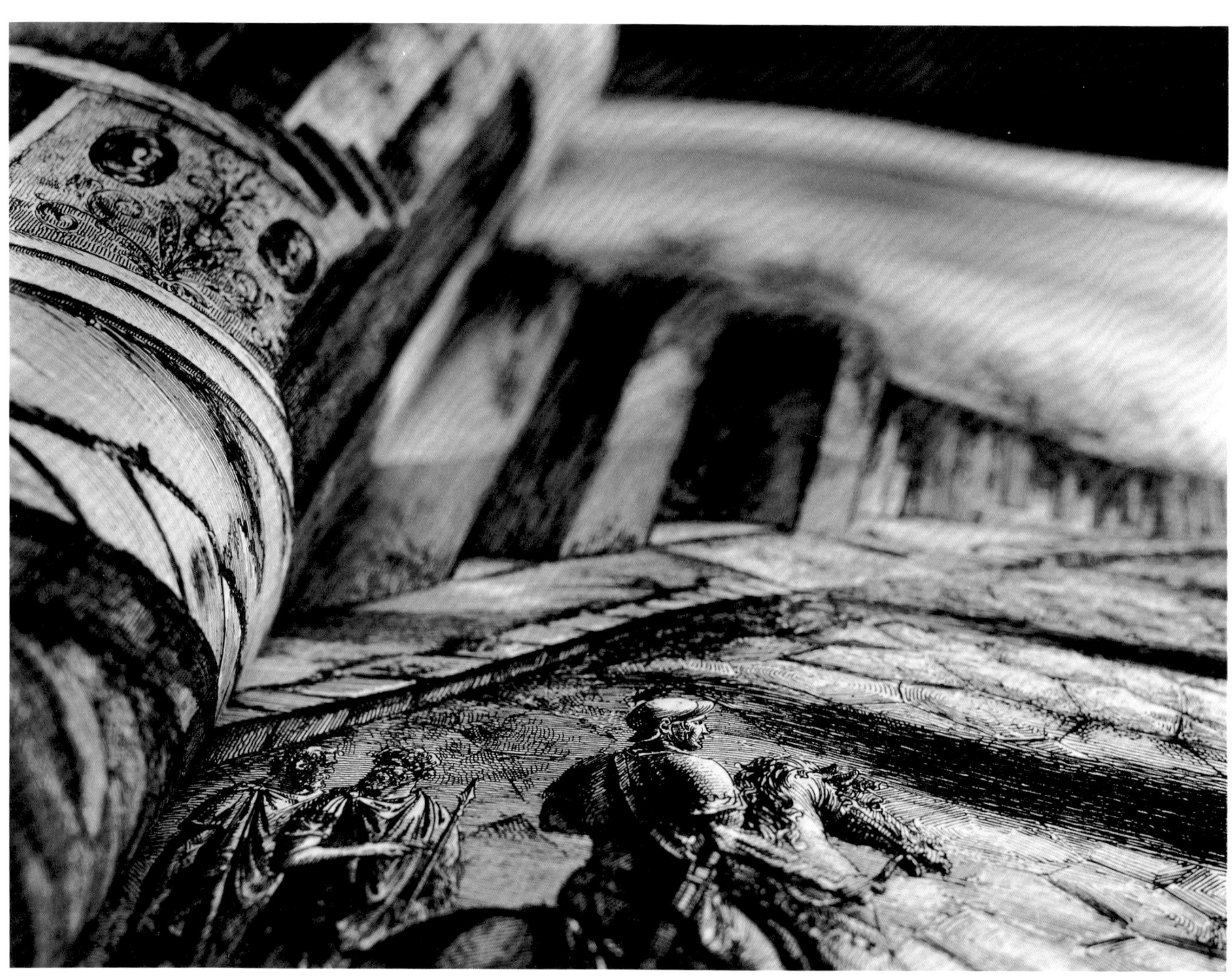

Book: *Diversi Ornati Di Pompeia* by Piranesi #1, 1994

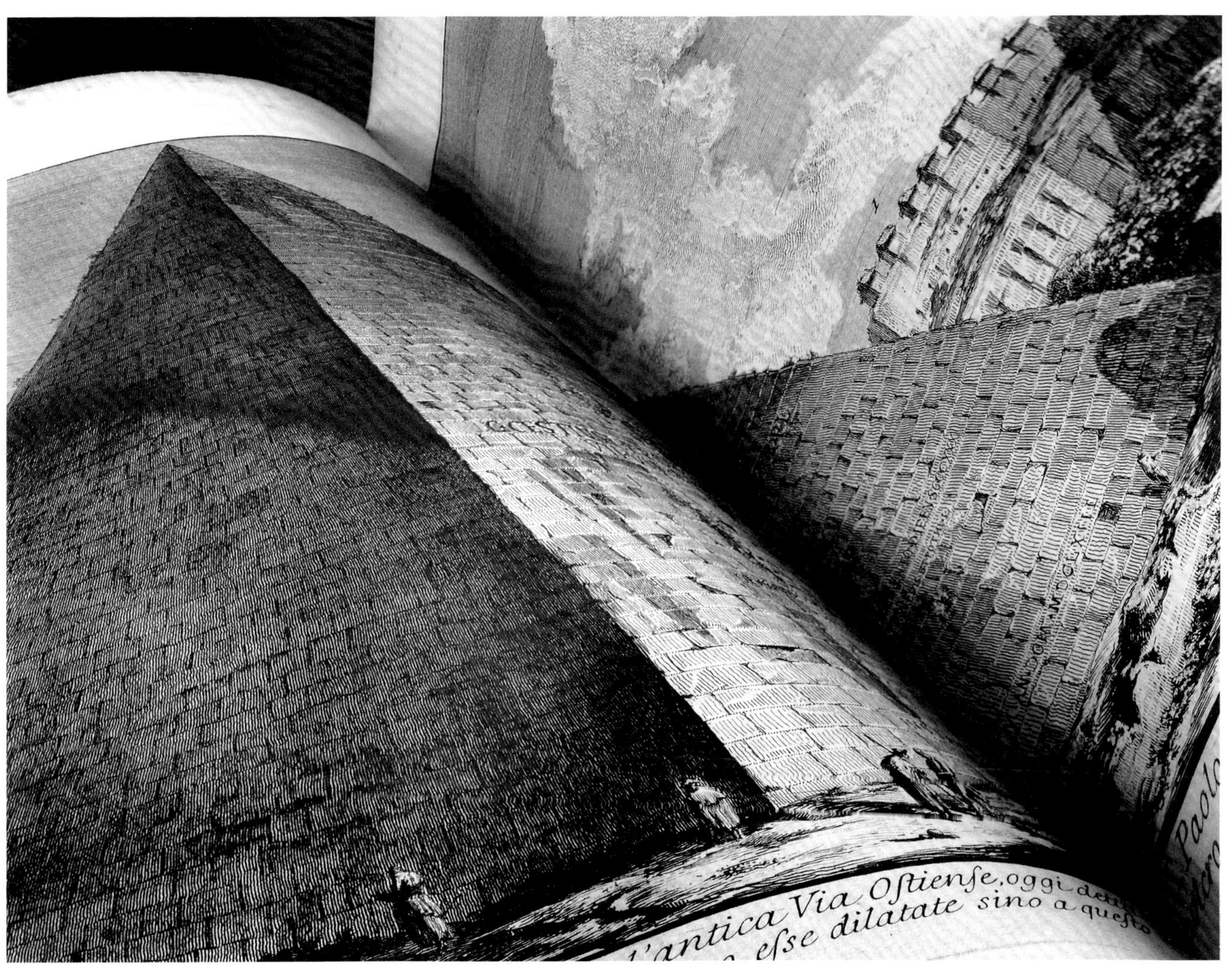

Book: *Le Antichita Romane* by Piranesi #1, 1994

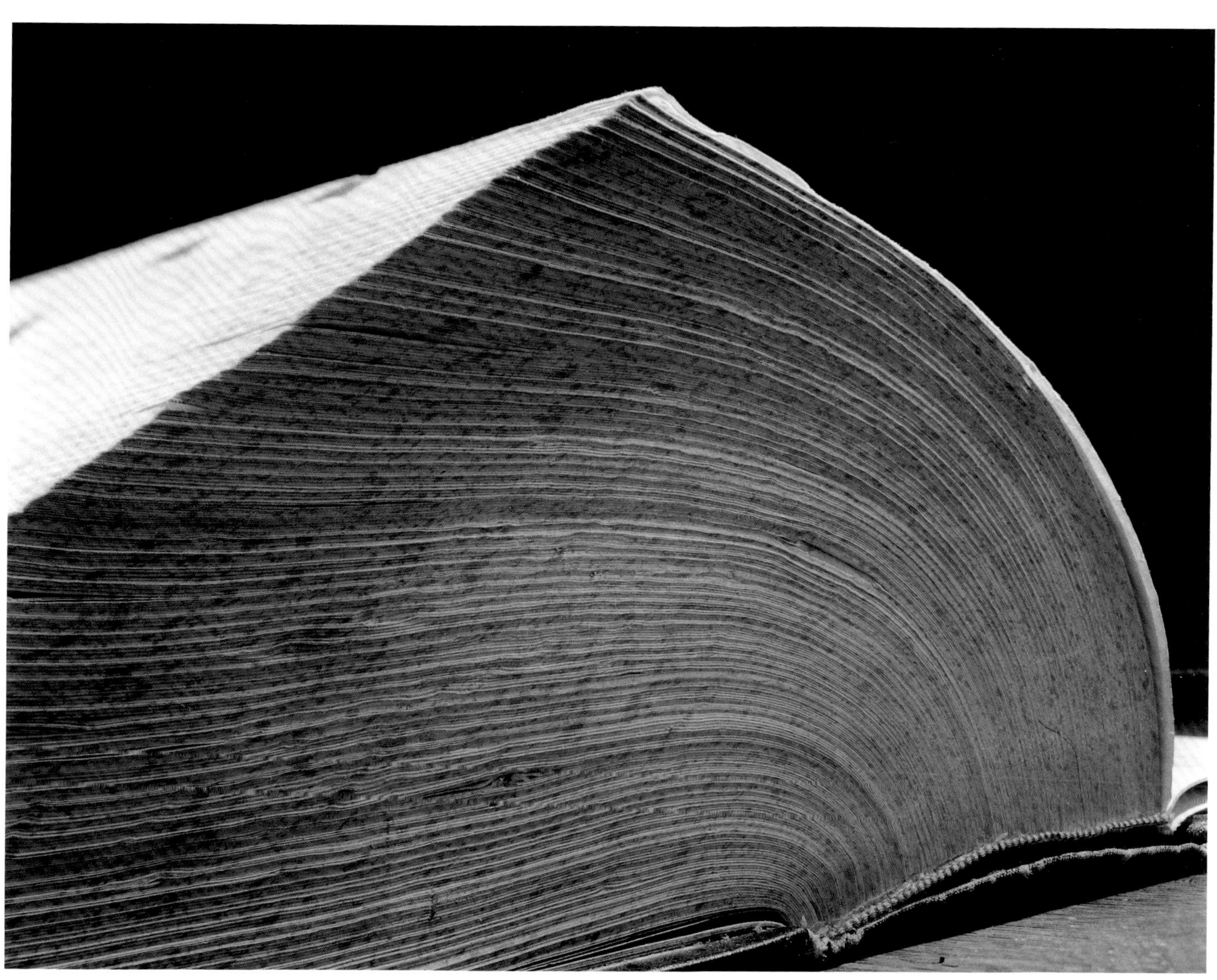

Dictionary, 1994

Abelardo Morell

Abelardo Morell has distinguished himself in the '90s as an artist of unique technical elegance and resourcefulness. Thoroughly exploiting the optical properties of the camera, he has taken photographs of homespun simplicity that demonstrate how this picture-making machine breaks down and reconstitutes the world on film via the binary code of black and white. Not only has he taken startling pictures unlike any others in the history of photography, he has done so within the confines of a "straight" aesthetic, without resorting to the stale tricks of surrealist collage or computerized postmodern manipulation.

The three distinct bodies of work that he has produced since the late '80s—his "camera obscura" images, studies of household objects, and pictures of pictures in books—share a common source that he shows no sign of exhausting. They portray domestic life from the visionary but utterly lucid perspective of a child in a way that restores conventional scenes and things to their original sensory-sharp scale, queer and dreamy texture, and pure awesomeness of being.

Born in Havana, Cuba, in 1948, Morell emigrated with his parents and sister to New York City at the age of fourteen. He attended Bowdoin College, where he studied Comparative Religion and for the first time took up photography in earnest. The camera became an instrument to express his bewildered sense of himself as a recent immigrant adrift in psychedelic America during the late '60s. Under the influence of Robert Frank's *The Americans,* he began a long apprenticeship as a street photographer who, although he later swore allegiance to the creed of the undoctored print, was at the time not above solarizing or toning his pictures for bizarre effects.

Morell's career is a stellar example of how, after a long period of study and imitation, an artist can unexpectedly erupt with a stream of novel ideas. After taking an M.F.A. from Yale in 1981, he began teaching photography at the Massachusetts College of Art in 1983 and married the independent filmmaker and producer, Lisa McElaney. He credits the birth of their son, Brady, in 1986, with the radical change that his work underwent in the late '80s. Housebound by fatherhood, he began to discover the potential for pictures of his new boundaries. He explored the floor with his son and found himself imagining the elements that make up a child's world at first glance and touch. His photograph of Brady sitting in a chair, as seen from the position of an even smaller entity, sparked a series of interior pictures. At the same time, on a sabbatical from teaching and eager to show his students the workings of a camera obscura when he returned to his duties, he devised a way to photograph the inverted image that appears when an aperture lets light into a sealed space. These "camera obscura" pictures that he produced after much trial and error are among his most heralded and quite unlike any pictures ever made.

Morell finds ordinary rooms and turns them into cameras. Taping black plastic over all the windows, he leaves one 3/8-inch hole, which provides the light for the picture. He then sets up his large-format camera on a tripod inside the room, focuses his lens on the walls opposite the windows, stops down for maximum depth of field, opens the shutter, and leaves the room. Each exposure takes about eight hours.

The photographs record the marriage of a domestic scene and the world beyond the window. Hostage to the whims of the weather, Morell can never predict how the outdoors will look as it slowly leaks into, combines with, and is photographed against the great indoors. For his earliest efforts, he chose the bedrooms of his house in Brookline, Massachusetts. But he has also produced a camera obscura of the Empire State Building and a seascape along the Atlantic coast.

In a related but separate manner, his pictures of objects around the home—kitchen utensils in water, the inside of a paper sack, his broken eye-glasses on the table—examine with a sophisticated naivite the animating presence of light in daily life. His ongoing series on the illustrations in children's books and art history tomes is similarly wide-eyed and shrewd. Morell has indirectly taken as his subject the means of manufacturing and reproducing images, and his own images of these images are no less strange and familiar and refreshing to think about. Seen at reading distance by the camera, pictures themselves become supremely odd cultural artefacts in which the gutters of a page or the reflective quality of ink can determine how we see the human face and body, or read the canon of art history. The basic act of leafing through and learning from books has never seemed more unnatural, contingent as it is on the peculiar and time-honored norms of publishing.

Morell received grants for these projects from the Cintas Foundation in 1992 and the Guggenheim Foundation in 1993. His work can be found in the permanent collections of the Museum of Modern Art and Metropolitan Museum of Art, New York, Art Institute of Chicago, Houston Museum of Fine Arts, the San Francisco Museum of Modern Art, Boston Museum of Fine Arts, Hallmark Photographic Collection in Kansas City, Missouri, and many other institutions.

He lives in Brookline, Massachusetts, with his wife, Lisa McElaney, and their two children, Brady and Laura.

—Richard B. Woodward

Technical information

Abelardo Morell has shot his photographs since 1986 with a 6 x 7 Fujica and a 4 x 5 Toyo view camera mounted with a 150 or 90mm wide-angle lens. He uses Tri-X film and prints on Ilford multi-grade paper.